Forgotten Light

For my mother,
Geraldine C. Callaghan
and to the memory of my
grand-daughter, Lily Páircéir

Forgotten Light

Memory Poems

Edited by
Louise C. Callaghan

A. & A. Farmar

Cover image: detail from 'Beachscape at Noon' by Eithne Jordan
Cover design by Alice Campbell
Text designed and set by A. & A. Farmar
Printed and bound by GraphyCems

ISBN 1-899047-84-0

First published in 2003 by
A. & A. Farmar
Beech House, 78 Ranelagh Village, Dublin 6, Ireland
Tel: + 353 1 496 3625 Fax: + 353 1 497 0107
Email: afarmar@iol.ie Web: farmarbooks.com

Editor's note

In reading, choosing and transcribing the poems in this collection, my life has been immeasurably enriched. The pleasure was enhanced by the responsiveness of seventy or so living poets who agreed to have their poems reprinted in this anthology. This personal contact with poets, from far and near, and their generosity, has warmed the work.

I feel a special gratitude to my friend Niall MacMonagle who travels the way with poets and poetry to an extraordinary degree. And to poet and friend, Susan Connolly, who over the years has been so generous. She introduced me to many of the poets included here whose works have become my favourite reading.

I would like to offer my thanks to many gifted translators. Thanks also to Eithne Jordan for allowing the use of her painting on the cover.

Louise C. Callaghan
October 2003

Contents

Foreword

The key to defining who we are, and establishing our personal identity and sense of worth, is memory; without memory we are non-persons living in a strange, barren limbo land.

When any of us look back over the past and remember how we were and what we did then we re-affirm who we are. Memory and emotion are interlinked, we are comforted, consoled, saddened, encircled by the past which has made us what we are today, special, unique, ourselves. This is very poignantly demonstrated by the poets in this collection of memory poems.

For someone with Alzheimer's Disease, however, this sense of self is eroded, for one of the first main symptoms of this disease is short-term memory loss which leaves people stranded between memories of early youth and the immediate moment, with a large barren void in between.

Life is dramatically and radically changed. When you can't remember mundane but essential things like where the toilet is, how to make a cup of tea, how to dress yourself or, more poignantly, when you are unable to recognise your nearest and dearest and when once familiar surroundings appear alien and strange, living is greatly curtailed and changed, creating many difficulties for the people themselves and for those who care for them.

The Alzheimer Society of Ireland, started in 1982, understands the many problems and emotive issues involved and seeks to address them.

As a first step we set up a number of support groups in Dublin; now there are 40 groups, spread all over the country, which meet once a month in the same venue led by persons with personal experience and special knowledge. They are places where carers can come together and voice their fears, anxieties, problems, in an understanding and helpful atmosphere, and can often act as a safety valve for those almost at the 'end of their tether'.

Another step forward came in 1989 with the opening of our first day care centre in Blackrock, Co. Dublin. We now operate 27 specialist day care centres nationwide. The ethos in these centres is positive with emphasis placed on what a person can still do rather than on what they cannot.

As memory is so compromised in Alzheimer's Disease one therapy we use in our centres is reminiscence therapy which works by tapping into those very early, still retained memories which are activated by the skilful use of memory triggers either verbal or tangible. It is a marvellous means for nurturing relationships, sustaining communication and enriching the lives of people experiencing the various disabilities, life restrictions and increasing social isolation which Alzheimer's Disease brings. It is of great assistance to both formal and informal carers, as knowing about a person's past illuminates our understanding of them in the present.

For those who cannot or do not wish to come to our day centres we have numerous home support and home care services spread over a wide area of the country. At the heart of all this hub-bub of activity lie 27 branches with their dedicated, hardworking members, all ably assisted by our professional staff.

The worried, anxious and depressed keep our free phone helpline busy every day, Monday to Friday. They are seeking reassurance, advice, information and very often simply a sympathetic listening ear.

Predictions for the future as the population ages is for an increase in the number of dementia cases and consequently increased need for our services. Now, even in our 21st year, there will be no resting on our laurels; we must keep on expanding, moving forward to meet the increasing need. Great plans for the future are being put in place.

Many shades of emotion surround Alzheimer's Disease, sadness, anger, a sense of loss, as well as joy and good times remembered— emotions which are echoed back from the pages of this collection of memory poems, sensitively selected by Louise C. Callaghan.

The ASI is indebted to the contributors, editor and publishers for making the Alzheimer Society the beneficiary of the proceeds from this book of memory poems. To all involved our grateful thanks.

Winifred Bligh
Founder Member and Member of the Board of Directors,
The Alzheimer Society of Ireland

Introduction

Louise C. Callaghan

Memory is that bridge which takes us back to what was lost or forgotten. In *Forgotten Light*, we read of many aspects of that journey.

There are poems which remember parents, grandparents, daughter, brother. Wislawa Szymborska, the Polish poet, writes of her dead parents:

> Memory at last has what it sought.
> My mother has been found, my father glimpsed.

Enda Wyley remembers her mother/storyteller in 'Dish of a Moon'. There are poems here about remembered people, both beloved and otherwise. In 'Anthem', Rita Ann Higgins writes:

> I wouldn't give an inch,
> you wouldn't give an inch.
> Hammer and tongs our anthem.

And, of course, there is the remembered self as in Medbh McGuckian's 'Open Rose':

> I have grown inside words
> Into a state of unbornness,
> An open rose on all sides
> Has spoken as far as it can.

Memory has given us poems about remembered times and places. For example, in 'The Big House', Anne Haverty's ironic lament is for a people lost in time, where only their trees remain.

> These doomy trees avenge Kilcash.
> The roof is fallen into the hall.

Sherman Alexie, the Spokane/Coeur d'Alene poet, remembers the history of generations of his people on the Spokane Indian reservation in 'Indian Boy Love Song'. In Susan Connolly's poem, 'Heartwood', memory is stored in the tree's interior:

> So I began to unwind
> my years for you,
> to let you see as far into myself
> as I can remember.

A particular memory allows us share in the poet's life-story. Macdara Woods' moving poem, 'November', chosen from his sequence of poems, *The Nightingale Water*, follows the progress of his mother's last illness and

at the unexplored end
of Ranelagh—

his own repossession of childhood.

William Wordsworth is the poet of things past, and 'emotion recollected in tranquillity.' 'Surprised by joy', written quite late in his life was, he says, 'suggested by my daughter, Catherine, long after her death'. Angela Greene also commemorates a dead child in 'Elegy'. Many of the poems chosen are obituary memory poems, for the recently departed, for friends ripped from time. Memory is essentially about time and the human mind. Edith Södergran, the Finno-Swedish poet who died so young, plays with the unknowable concept of time:

> Time—convertress, time—destructress, time—
>   enchantress,
> do you come with new schemes, a thousand tricks
>   to offer me existence

Roz Cowman and Walt Whitman, in their distinct ways, explore imaginary memories. Cowman, in 'Dream of the Red Chamber', traces her way back to an existence in the hill of her mother's womb. Whitman remembers an imagined friend of his youth.

> I have somewhere surely lived a life of joy with you . . .
> I am to wait, I do not doubt I am to meet you again,
> I am to see to it that I do not lose you.

Minnie Bruce Pratt's erotic love poem, 'Done', explores the way memory has its part in fantasy and masturbation.

To remember pre-supposes our forgetting. E.E. Cummings, in his epitaph-like poem, plays with this concept of remembering and forgetting—the seek and ye shall find wisdom—turned upside down: 'remember seek(forgetting find)'. It reminds us of Emily Dickinson's 'You cannot make Remembrance grow'. 'In School', by Noel Monahan, associates this habit of memory with forgetfulness.

> We remembered and forgot,
> We repeated, remembered and forgot,
> We recited and forgot,

And infinitely sad John Clare's poem, 'I Am' from the Asylum in Northampton:

> I am: yet what I am none cares or knows,
>   My friends forsake me like a memory lost;.

Leland Bardwell in 'No Return' says it is too late, that memory is, at best, a belated effort. In another love poem, 'Distances', Eavan

Boland explores memory as a kind of nostalgia, where far off fields are tattered remnants.

In certain of these poems memory is a testament. A *memorare*. Paul Celan, who lost his entire family in the Nazi death camps, is dark on the theme of memory. In 'Corona', he wishes for what a critic called 'the mantle of oblivion' while acknowledging the imperative of memory. 'All things are unforgotten', he wrote in a letter to Nelly Sachs.

Loneliness is captured in some of the poems in *Forgotten Light*. Charles Simic, in 'Gray-Headed Schoolchildren', writes

> Every old man is alone
> In this classroom . . .

Antonia Pozzi discovers the lyric potential of memory in 'Death of a Season' which articulates a kind of longing:

> All night long it rained
> on the memories of summer.

But you will read too of indelible first love, of passionate encounter and of happy day-dreaming. Take the Whitmanesque poem by Cathal Ó Searcaigh 'Do Jack Kerouac':

> Ag sioscadh trí do shaothar anocht tháinig leoithne
>   na cuimhne chugam ó gach leathanach.
> Athmhúsclaíodh m'óige is mhothaigh mé ag eirí
>   ionam an *beat* brionglóideach a bhí ag
>   déanamh aithris ort i dtús na seachtóidí.

so happily translated here by Sara Berkeley:

> Thumbing through your work tonight the aroma
>   of memories came from every page.
> My youth rewoke and I felt rising in me the
>   dreamy beat that imitated you at the start of the 70's.

History speaks to memory in Caitríona O'Reilly's poem 'Nineteen Eighty-Four' with its astute sense of Irish gender politics. The Greek goddess Mnemosyne, whose name means Memory, is the mother of the Muses. Perhaps the Hungarian poet Ágnes Nemes Nagy addresses her in 'The Sleeping Form':

> Speak, speak finally wherever
> in your mute dream.

The last word belongs to Shakespeare's *Twelfth Night* where, wistfully, the clown Feste sings to himself before the play finishes:

> When that I was and a little tiny boy,
> With hey, ho, the wind and the rain . . .

Memory poems

FLEUR ADCOCK

Outwood

Milkmaids, buttercups, ox-eye daisies,
white and yellow in the tall grass:
I fought my way to school through flowers—
bird's-foot trefoil, clover, vetch—
my sandals all smudged with pollen,
seedy grass-heads caught in my socks.

At school I used to read, mostly,
and hide in the shed at dinnertime,
writing poems in my notebook.
'Little fairies dancing,' I wrote,
and 'Peter and I, we watch the birds fly,
high in the sky, in the evening.'

Then home across the warm common
to tease my little sister again:
'I suppose you thought I'd been to school:
I've been to work in the bicycle shop.'
Mummy went to a real job
every day, on a real bicycle;

Doris used to look after us.
She took us for a walk with a soldier,
through the damp ferns in the wood
into a clearing like a garden,
rosy-pink with beds of campion,
herb-robert, lady's smock.

The blackberry briars were pale with blossom.
I snagged my tussore dress on a thorn;
Doris didn't even notice.
She and the soldier lay on the grass;
he leaned over her pink blouse
and their voices went soft and round, like petals.

SHERMAN ALEXIE

Indian Boy Love Songs

1
Everyone I have lost
in the closing of a door
the click of the lock

is not forgotten, they
do not die but remain
within the soft edges
of the earth, the ash

of house fires and cancer
in sin and forgiveness
huddled under old blankets

dreaming their way into
my hands, my heart
closing tight like fists.

2
I never spoke
the language
of the old women

visiting my mother
in winters so cold
they could freeze
the tongue whole.

I never held my head
to their thin chests
believing in the heart.

Indian women, forgive me.
I grew up distant
and always afraid.

3
I remember when I told
my cousin
she was more beautiful

than any white girl
I had ever seen.
She kissed me then
with both lips, a tongue

that tasted clean and un-
clean at the same time
like the river which divides

the heart of my heart, all
the beautiful white girls on one side,
my beautiful cousin on the other.

4
I remember when my father would leave,
drinking,
for weeks. My mother would tell me

the dream he needed
most
was the dream that frightened him
more

than any stranger ever could.
I
would wait by my window, dreaming

bottles
familiar in my hands, not my father's, always
empty.

NUALA ARCHER

Riding Out a Storm

There is no need for a home.
When raindrops pound the earth
to dough and lash the hollyhock
back and forth through a great arc,

I cling to the underside
of leaves and wait for the typhoon
to whip itself still. I watch
clouds caricature ancestors—

such mounds the fluff makes
of them! And then the clouds
sift toward me like broken clocks,
like fragile ferries.

When every feather of water has
fallen from its perch, I am going
to climb some unheeding face and watch
eagles stress the teetering horizon.

INGEBORG BACHMANN

A Kind of Loss

Translated by Mark Anderson

Used together: seasons, books, a piece of music.
The keys, teacups, bread basket, sheets and a bed.
A hope chest of words, of gestures, brought back, used, used up.
A household order maintained. Said. Done. And always a hand
  was there.

I've fallen in love with winter, with a Viennese septet, with
  summer.
With village maps, a mountain nest, a beach and a bed.
Kept a calender cult, declared promises irrevocable,
bowed before something, was pious to a nothing

(—to a folded newspaper, cold ashes, the scribbled piece of paper),
fearless in religion, for our bed was the church.

From my lake view arose my inexhaustible painting.
From my balcony I greeted entire peoples, my neighbors.
By the chimney fire, in safety, my hair took on its deepest hue.
The ringing at the door was the alarm for my joy.

It's not you I've lost,
but the world.

The Japanese Kite

My father bellowed at the sea, livid with himself, the tides and God knows what. Bald, demented Neptune. Rake for a trident, he battered the gleaming coils of weed, scraped them off the sand, drove them into a vast, snaky heap. Nearby, my son played planes, paying no heed to his strange grandpa or the luminous sea. Then I took out the Japanese kite. The child seized the bright scrap and flung it into air. Up, up it flew, energy bird. The unspooling cord hopped on the sands while still my father roared, slapped his own pate with angry hands. When the boy went off to chase the waves, I wrapped the kitestring round my father's bony fingers.

The kite tugged
And pulled.
A soft pulse of air
Escaped my father's lips.
Hooked, I thought.
Inch by inch,
His old eyes
Followed the line,
Up, up
Towards the dancing speck
Up, up
To the sky.
Then his ancient mouth
Creaked
To a smile,
His back straightened.
That day,
Connected again
By a cord,
My dying father
Sailed that Japanese kite
Into the night.

No Return

They tried to recapture
the days of Leonard Cohen.
Dylan, the Beatles
as they downed a bottle of Bush,
sang unmusically, fell
into the bed.

It was a belated effort—
two desperadoes on a sinking ship
no pirate of passion
to storm the bulwark.
They laughed at last,
remembering the mornings
of Black Russian cigarettes.

The man I knew

He climbed on his life,
hands ragged, winter-blown eyes;
space revolved around his world,
a million lights were lost in thought—
it wasn't the dark that mattered.

The man I knew
threw his life in the water;
the man I knew surfaced and gasped,
he was survivor, kicking the boards
of the boardwalk, grabbing the rails
for a long haul
back to the real world.

His colours came through.
In his single room
no one held him as he wept
and he was glad of no one.

Without sight, he was
ready for life; kicked dust at the stars,
swung with a measure of hope,
made no bones of it.

All that winter
his letters fluttered to my letterbox;
although I broke the hold, I turned aside,
and read them all, and cried.

On goes
the hungry scissors up our paper lives.
The whole splits, the halves
roll back alone. High on his life
something else, different and good,
can begin. Across his sky
a million lights go on,
his palm ghosts the back of my neck,
his memories reach out and back,
he is travelling light.

EAVAN BOLAND

Distances

The radio is playing downstairs in the kitchen.
The clock says eight and the light says
winter. You are pulling up your hood against a bad morning.

Don't leave, I say. Don't go without telling me
the name of that song. You call it back to me from the stairs:
'I Wish I Was In Carrickfergus'

and the words open out with emigrant grief the way the streets
of a small town open out in
memory: salt-loving fuchsias to one side and

a market in full swing on the other with
linen for sale and tacky apples and a glass and wire hill
of spectacles on a metal tray. The front door bangs

and you're gone. I will think of it all morning while a fine
drizzle closes in, making the distances
fiction: not of that place but this and of how

restless we would be, you and I, inside the perfect
music of that basalt and sandstone
coastal town. We would walk the streets in

the scentless afternoon of a ballad measure,
longing to be able
to tell each other that the starched lace and linen of

adult handkerchiefs scraped your face and left your tears
falling; how the apples were mush inside the crisp sugar
shell and the spectacles out of focus.

LUCY BRENNAN

Mullaghbawn 1950

for Nellie Mac

A breathing space
tucked into the slopes of Slieve Gullion
one day slipping into another
and no one noticing

The Border's a hurdle
but the cousins' house over at Jonesborough
straddles it
obviates the customs post

I'm searching for ancestors
up in the hills
and fireplaces or an Aga cooker
with tea on the hob
that takes you talking overnight
into the next afternoon
Stay awhile . . . There's no rush
everything will keep

Old memories
thumbing a broken-backed book of poetry
my mother was given
before I was born

Thoughts covered in wit
the only thing that's angular

There's much more maybe
boiling beneath
but if so I'm young and only a visitor
no one would heap troubles
on a guest

C ATHERINE B YRON

The Blue Darkness

I'm reading *Bavarian Gentians* and it's not death I see, or
  Persephone's shotgun marriage in the fields of Enna. No.

It's the long coarse throats of gentians gross as pitcher
  plants, lapped in the rangy grass of La Chartreuse.

Jos is wearing indigo jeans, Bavarian gentian jeans. His
  presence is marinading my innards to soup. I lust
  luxuriously and on the quiet. He has no idea.

There are five of us on the valley road to La Chartreuse,
  down near the riverbed where the woodsorrel flowers are
  pale as shock, and forget-me-nots shake dull stars into the
  stream. Only the gentians hold the deep dye colourfast in
  their grassy spools.

A thin fire runs through my limbs. I am paler than wood-
  land grass, paler than sorrel. I am seventeen.

LOUISE C. CALLAGHAN

Foal

A memory, singular
star-like burns

from afar it falls
towards you—

a forgotten light.
A chestnut mare

alone in the meadow,
when you turned once more

no time no hour

the foal unfolding
from long-ago grass.

MARY ROSE CALLAN

Replay

Let me take it back, that day
with you on the bus to Bundoran,
shake it like a cloth
at April's door where everything
seems possible; a chance
to give you the window seat
beside me, your teenage daughter.

This time I won't shrink
from the tweed skirt
you wore on days out, even in sun,
or build a wall of sugar lumps
between us on the café table
knocking it down
whenever you speak.

We'll pass Ben Bulben again,
half home on the last bus
unshaken sand
in folds of the skirt
you arranged on stone
as I watched
from my corner of the beach.

SIOBHÁN CAMPBELL

Recall

Pitiless, disease and hunger spread.
Our people fled. We live now
knowing we are those
who bullied, stole and beat.
O'Hare, Kelly, Campbell, Helly—
take heed for we survived.
Our curse is that we've understood
what hurts: we know the will
that curls a feeding smile;
we have been merciless and thrived.

Timbre

A word does not head out alone.
It is carried about the way something essential,
a blade, say, or a wooden bowl,
is brought from here to there when there is work to be done.
Sometimes, after a long journey,
it is pressed into a different service.

A tree keeps its record of years
and of the temper of years
well hidden until after death.

After the timber has been sawn
rough rings release the song of the place—
droughts, good summers, long frosts—
the way pain and joy unlock in a voice.

PHILIP CASEY

Notes Towards Old Music

for Pearse Hutchinson

A bell struck by a fingernail
A whale's deep song
The hum of a powerline
The groan of a stationary train.

PAUL CELAN

Corona

Translated by Michael Hamburger

Autumn eats its leaf out of my hand: we are friends.
From the nuts we shell time and we teach it to walk:
then time returns to the shell.

In the mirror it's Sunday,
in dream there is room for sleeping,
our mouths speak the truth.

My eye moves down to the sex of my loved one:
we look at each other,
we exchange dark words,
we love each other like poppy and recollection,
we sleep like wine in the conches,
like the sea in the moon's blood ray.

We stand by the window embracing, and people look up from the street:
it is time they knew!
It is time the stone made an effort to flower,
time unrest had a beating heart.
It is time it were time.

It is time.

John Clare

I Am

The Asylum, Northampton

I am: yet what I am none cares or knows,
  My friends forsake me like a memory lost;
I am the self-consumer of my woes,
  They rise and vanish in oblivious host,
Like shades in love and death's oblivion lost;
And yet I am, and live with shadows tost

Into the nothingness of scorn and noise,
  Into the living sea of waking dreams,
Where there is neither sense of life nor joys,
  But the vast shipwreck of my life's esteems;
And e'en the dearest—that I loved the best—
Are strange—nay, rather stranger than the rest.

I long for scenes where man has never trod;
  A place where woman never smiled or wept;
There to abide with my creator, G O D,
  And sleep as I in childhood sweetly slept:
Untroubling and untroubled where I lie;
The grass below— above the vaulted sky.

AUSTIN CLARKE

From Mnemosyne Lay in Dust

XVIII

Rememorised, Maurice Devane
Went out, his future in every vein,
The Gate had opened. Down Steeven's Lane
The high wall of the Garden, to right
Of him, the Fountain with a horse-trough,
Illusions had become a story.
There was the departmental storey
Of Guinness's, God-given right
Of goodness in every barrel, tun,
They averaged. Upon that site
Of shares and dividends in sight
Of Watling Street and the Cornmarket,
At Number One in Thomas Street
Shone in the days of the ballad-sheet,
The house in which his mother was born.

SUSAN CONNOLLY

Heartwood

Am I the familiar tree
of your childhood
you sometimes sat beside
alone and happy?

Or am I a mysterious tree
you never encountered before,
making you curious
about me?

Whichever I am—
when you first knew me
my life lay hidden in rings
you couldn't yet decipher.

So I began to unwind
my years for you,
to let you see as far into myself
as I can remember.

On a night when stars hurt
my eyes, I saw
my thoughts broken, scattered
around me like fallen leaves.

You sat here,
and my voice cracked
as I tried to release
another part of my life.

On a day when the sun shone
we went by the river;
the sun listened to our talk:
curious, it followed us home.

Poor Lily

'Far away places, with strange-sounding
names, far away over the sea . . .'

Remember the song, Lily?
You used to sing it when you were young
and dream how one day you would go over
the sea and find out for yourself.

'Poor Lily, left on the shelf',
your family said. 'Never found a man
to take her to his bed. It all went
wrong inside her head. Poor dead Lily!'

Poor Lily. How strange and far away
your family were. How peculiar.

Roz Cowman

Dream of the Red Chamber

Red tides have filled
the estuary; dykes
are down; the land
of the two canals
is gone.

Old hill, if I tread
stepping-stones of black
bungalows back to the first
threshold, the dream
of a red room,

will you accept
my journey as a rite
of passage, and absorb me

as the hare mother absorbs
her foetus children
into her blood

when spring is stillborn,
and late frosts
salt the earth?

E.E. CUMMINGS

in time of daffodils(who know

in time of daffodils(who know
the goal of living is to grow)
forgetting why,remember how

in time of lilacs who proclaim
the aim of waking is to dream,
remember so(forgetting seem)

in time of roses(who amaze
our now and here with paradise)
forgetting if,remember yes

in time of all sweet things beyond
whatever mind may comprehend,
remember seek(forgetting find)

and in a mystery to be
(when time from time shall set us free)
forgetting me,remember me

Return

The train shot through the dark.
Hedges leapt across the window-pane.
Trees belled in foliage were stranded,
Inarticulate with rain.
A blur of lighted farm implied
The evacuated countryside.

I am appalled by its emptiness.
Every valley glows with pain
As we run like a current through;
Then the memories darken again.
In this Irish past I dwell
Like sound implicit in a bell.

The train curves round a river,
And how tenderly its gouts of steam
Contemplate the nodding moon
The waters from the clouds redeem.
Two hours from Belfast
I am snared in my past.

Crusts of light lie pulsing
Diamanté with the rain
At the track's end. Amazing!
I am in Derry once again.
Once more I turn to greet
Ground that flees from my feet.

CELIA DE FRÉINE

Picnic i reilig sa Bhílearúis

Tugaimid faoi deara cé atá as láthair.
Básaithe? Gan ar a gcumas
aghaidh a thabhairt ar athaontú eile?
Leatar brait bhoird, roinntear béigil,
is a luaithe a chasann an garda thart,
rithimid trí ghoirt chuig na fothraigh
ina mbíodh cónaí orainn, tráth.

Cuardaíonn mo mhac seoda idir na cláir,
ach malartaíodh gach maoineach cheana féin
le linn geilleagair chomh dubh
leis an múrabhán a thug an matalang leis.
Is í mo mháthair an bhean sa ghúna dearg
atá ag bualadh a cloiginn i gcoinne an chlaí,
ag caoineadh na mbó nach féidir léi a chrú .

Celia de Fréine

Picnic in a cemetery in Belarus

We note who's missing. Dead?
Unable to face another reunion?
Tablecloths are spread, bagels
shared, and the minute
the guard turns his back,
we race across fields
to ruins that once were home.

My son searches between boards
for mementoes, but every possession
has long since been bartered in an economy
as black as the cloud that brought disaster.
That woman in red whom you see
beating her head against a fence is my mother.
She weeps for the cows she cannot milk.

GREG DELANTY

To My Mother, Eileen

I'm threading the eye
   of the needle for you again. That is
my specially appointed task, my
     gift that you gave me. Ma, watch me slip this
      camel of words through. Yes,
rich we are still even if your needlework
   has long since gone with the rag-and-bone man
     and Da never came home one day, our Dan.
   Work Work Work. Lose yourself in work.
    That's what he'd say.
       Okay okay.
Ma, listen I can hear the sticks of our fire spit
   like corn turning into popcorn
     with the brown insides of rotten teeth. We sit
in our old Slieve Mish house. Norman is just born.
   He's in the pen.
I raise the needle to the light and lick the thread
    to stiffen the limp words. I
peer through the eye, focus and put everything out of my head.
    I shut my right eye and thread.
I'm important now, a likely lad, instead
   of the amadán at Dread School. I have the eye
    haven't I, the knack?
   I'm Prince Threader. I missed it that try.
    Concentrate. Concentrate. Enough yackety yak.
There, there, Ma, look, here's the threaded needle back.

EMILY DICKINSON

You cannot make Remembrance grow

You cannot make Remembrance grow
When it has lost its Root—
The tightening the Soil around
And setting it upright
Deceives perhaps the Universe
But not retrieves the Plant—
Real Memory, like Cedar Feet
Is shod with Adamant—
Nor can you cut Remembrance down
When it shall once have grown—
In Iron Buds will sprout anew
However overthrown—

At Every Window A Different Season

I remember a house
where we sat to watch
the days pass;
hour by hour.
The changing of the light
on mountain and lake.
The year's passage
in an afternoon.
At every window
a different season.

Bog and high grass
climbed the mountains
where sheep lay strewn
like white rocks,
cloud catching in their horns.
There were geese on the boreen,
cows in the hedgerows.
A church spire
and the ocean
at the foot of the garden.

On clear nights
stars shimmered
like cut glass
in the immensity of sky
that wrapped itself
and silence
end to end of the sleeping fields.

In winter
the roar of wind
drowned speech.
Walls shook and timber.
Wave upon wave
rocked our bed,
a currach at anchor
on the open sea.

I remember
a half door
thrown wide upon waking.
Hay stacks on the front lawn.
In summer
wild flowers rampant;
iris, primrose, foxglove.
And in the pools of sunshine after rain,
a table and chairs
of wrought iron
set out for late breakfast.

A garden adrift
between mist
and heat haze.
Palm trees,
fuchsia,
mallow.
And the wandering pathways
that led to the sea,
paved with orange flags
we carried stone by stone
from the most westerly strand
in the western world.

A house
full of cats and cooking.
Hanging baskets from the rafters;
plants in the baskets
and cats on the rafters
or sun bathing
under wide shaded pottery lamps.
A sailor's hammock,
a hearth and crane,
armchairs drawn to the fire.
Coffee on the stove,
wine on the table.
Music at three o'clock in the morning.

I remember a house
where we sat
to watch the days pass
hour by hour.
The changing of light
over mountain and lake.
The passage of a year
in an afternoon.
At every window
a different season.

CAROL ANN DUFFY

Stafford Afternoons

Only there, the afternoons could suddenly pause
and when I looked up from lacing my shoe
a long road held no one, the gardens were empty,
an ice-cream van chimed and dwindled away.

On the motorway bridge, I waved at windscreens,
oddly hurt by the blurred waves back, the speed.
So I let a horse in the noisy field sponge at my palm
and invented, in colour, a vivid lie for us both.

In a cul-de-sac, a strange boy threw a stone.
I crawled through a hedge into long grass
at the edge of a small wood, lonely and thrilled.
The green silence gulped once and swallowed me whole.

I knew it was dangerous. The way the trees
drew sly faces from light and shade, the wood
let out its sticky breath on the back of my neck,
and flowering nettles gathered spit in their throats.

Too late. *Touch,* said the long-haired man
who stood, legs apart, by a silver birch
with a living, purple root in his hand. The sight
made sound rush back; birds, a distant lawnmower,

his hoarse, frightful endearments as I backed away
then ran all the way home; into a game
where children scattered and shrieked
and time fell from the sky like a red ball.

PAUL DURCAN

The Voice of Eden

for Colm on your eleventh birthday

Playing golf aged eleven
In Ballybunnion in the rain;
Playing a seven iron and not being able
To see the hole and pitching up
Pin high! *Pin high!*
Seeking to emulate my father—
His swing, his sexy swing,
His Christy O'Connor slouch;
Trudging after him into nightfall.

After our game
Instead of driving home
He drives up on to the cliff,
Parks the black Vauxhall Wyvern
At right angles to the castle wall
About to subside into the Atlantic ocean;
His front wheels on the cliff edge;
His headlights switched on high beam—
Spotlights on the spouting, snorting nostrils of the sea.

For what are we waiting here?
I dare not enquire.
I am scared.
I am thrilled.
Is he watching out for ships?
For smugglers, gunrunners?
For that giant in history whom he pines for—
Roger Casement?
From under the driver's seat
He plucks a transistor radio
Cuddling it in his lap,
Coaxing out of its knobs
The BBC Home Service.

In the night in the rain
Through static
Like two silhouetted
Samurai in a canoe
On the brink of a thirty-foot wave
We listen to the voice of Eden
Trot across the ocean,
Black hooves shod in silver:
'I have to tell you that we are on the brink
Of a crisis grave as World War II.
By his criminal annexation of the Suez Canal
Colonel Nasser seeks to emulate
Hitler's annexation of Czechoslovakia.
Her Majesty's Government is at war with Egypt.'

We crouch in silence, Daddy and I,
A pair of fugitives,
Creatures of euphoria
And of blame,
Appalled.
Enchanted by
The voice of Eden
In Ballybunnion in the rain.

PETER FALLON

Another Anniversary

You turn
hearing the joy
of football
in the yard.
You yearn
for that footfall
of the lost,
the scarred.

Again, again
and again
you feel the sten-
gun attack
of that 'What if?'
and that 'What then?'
Well, then
he'd be a boy

who's ten.

LAWRENCE FERLINGHETTI

From Pictures of the Gone World

26.

Reading Yeats I do not think
                              of Ireland
but of midsummer New York
                              and of myself back then
        reading that copy I found
                              on the Thirdavenue El

        the El
                with its flyhung fans
        and its signs reading
                SPITTING IS FORBIDDEN

        the El
                careening thru its thirdstory world
        with its thirdstory people
                        in their thirdstory doors
looking as if they had never heard
                              of the ground

        an old dame
                    watering her plant
or a joker in a straw
                    putting a stickpin in his peppermint tie
and looking just like he had nowhere to go
                              but coneyisland
        or an undershirted guy
                        rocking in his rocker
watching the El pass by
                as if he expected it to be different
        each time

Reading Yeats I do not think
                            of Arcady
and of its woods which Yeats thought dead
                            I think instead
        of all the gone faces
                    getting off at midtown places
    with their hats and their jobs
            and of that lost book I had
                    with its blue cover and its white inside
where a pencilhand had written
                    HORSEMAN, PASS BY!

TESS GALLAGHER

For Yvonne

(Yvonne McDonagh-Gaffney)

Swept to her shoulders and out of the house—
the boys' sweaters, Granny's cardigan—that way
she had as a girl of borrowing
until we forgot to own. Now we coax her back
like a favorite garment that bears her scent,
laughter unravelling, like water breeze
pensive as a bride. How can she be
so everywhere and gone? Just like her to
store up warmth for us, stretching memory
like a sleeve until we are reshaped
by her absence. Coming upon *her* boat
marooned there on shore at Lough Arrow
is such wistfulness toward life
we know enough to turn it over,
climb in, let her hold us across the water.

ELIZABETH GRAINGER

The Good X

Her arrow is ready on the bowstring—
what will she aim for?
The neighborhood is already marked
all over, hers: the basketball hoop,
the stop sign, the neighbor's dog.

She's fifth in the family club,
not president or vice-, or secretary.
She's the Good X, for *be good and quiet*,
but she is all growls now, and dirt-smeared,
with hair now cherry, now blue raspberry

from Kool-Aid powder mixed without sugar.
She's a sour stain of primary color
and she chews the ends of her hair.
Pulls back the bowstring, considers.
Next week she'll be eleven.

Her pirate's reign will end with September;
all the alleys will return to strangeness,
her bow, to a stick and twine, her arrows,
to their shoebox den. A bath will wash away
all her markings, and rain, her territory.

ROBERT GREACEN

At Brendan Behan's Desk

Full seven years I've sat
And scribbled at this desk:
Cards, letters, poems, autosnaps,
Diary entries, shopping lists,
While Beatrice down below hoarded
Memories of Brendan in a clutter
Of paintings, posters, photos,
With for company two dogs.

To Brendan's ghost I must confess
My orderly grey days.
At moments I'd like to be out
Emptying glasses in the pubs
Of Dublin town, blarneying
To actors, poets, drunks,
Then taxi-ing back to *Cuig*
Not earlier than 3 a.m.,
Rousing the solid citizens,
Telling an uncaring world
How 'that old triangle
Went jingle, jangle
Along the banks of the Royal Canal.'

Instead, I sit at Brendan's desk,
Reading, scribbling, drinking coffee,
A Protestant without a horse.

ANGELA GREENE

Elegy

November, and my dead
crowd me. New-born,
you died before I saw you.

O, these years without you.
Yet you are always with me—
the words of a sad song
I can not complete.

Your infant limbs curl
in these syllables. You sleep
safe in sheets of soft white.

In other women's babies I look
for you. I pick among shells
for one fragment of you.

                    In the grass,
or high in the buds of Spring
where I almost hear you,
the wind shifts,
and its cry opens in blue air.

In the places children gather
I search and find, again and again,
that strange emptiness.

Asleep I see you, whole-limbed,
tall, running in the wind—
but awake the dream has kept you . . .

And you are where I must learn
to leave you, safe
with the dead. November,
old memories fret,
and my dead crowd me.

THOM GUNN

Memory Unsettled

Your pain still hangs in air,
Sharp motes of it suspended;
The voice of your despair—
That also is not ended:

When near your death a friend
Asked you what he could do,
'Remember me,' you said.
We will remember you.

Once when you went to see
Another with a fever
In a like hospital bed,
With terrible hothouse cough
And terrible hothouse shiver
That soaked him and then dried him,
And you perceived that he
Had to be comforted,

You climbed in there beside him
And hugged him plain in view,
Though you were sick enough,
And had your own fears too.

Washing

I remember that gaunt house,
mud to the door,
filled crack in the gable end,
work-clothes on the line (dark, weighty, shapeless),
the sound of water running
through gaps and dripping places,
down the shine of the road,
seeping among the rushes.
Then the gleam of wet roof-slates
in the hopelessly radiant light,
and the rose-coloured nightdress,
loud as a birth,
hung with those drab vestments—
it's a woman farms that land—
Her tender life
moves in the wet wind against the mountain.

ANNE LE MARQUAND HARTIGAN

from Leaving—

a section of *Now is a Moveable Feast*

i.

Strange, after years in a land
that was not your own
but taken to the bone.

Each path and dip
and where the trees part
and the shape

of the willow against the sky;
and why small birds return
to the same tree.

A shaft of scent
from the laden shrub
repeats its mood

onto the memory;
with pattern
it repatterns love
for a place.

Bidden to come
Bidden to leave.

This stretching space
this reach of sky,
this edge;

here land tilts over into sea
earth sea river merge
in passion, marriage,
and roaring war,
the mingling of foreign bloods.

Tilth of river
split and seared by salt tongues,
sand, soil, mud, a bond,

familiar war,
a give, a take,
as river pounds

a butting head
into the sea's breath,

rasping stone, easing into sand.
The sea's turbulent converse
with still land.

          ii.
After her leaving
was there no mark
left to show?

Footprints
in the mud go, fold,
ooze into nothing.

Long skirts brush
through dry leaves,
sweeping a little path.

Soon winds lift
and dart
tracing other
patterns over,

no sign
of the journey.

A light,
bobbing towards,
nearer
blinding,

then away, gone;
no trails on the air
yet,

everything
that touches a thing
changes it.

A love print on
the brain can
scald and bleach.

              A squawk of floorboards
              A chatter of cups.

Do trees remember
who passed under,
and when

as they push out
bud leaf flower
apple, and again

allow the sap to seep
back to the soil,
standing drained

for winter,
heart hardened
to the stiff breeze?

              Hand on the doorknob
              Hand on the bannister.

What is left
in rooms; a voice
to echo echo and
fade to nowhere?
Or are they nestling
with spiders

waiting to be spoken again?
Do walls soak in
through every pore

the slash of love,
the gush of birth,
the act of death?

Tidying Up

It used to be *my* room
full of lumber and the past;
all the memories of dead aunts,
of Mother, mothers,
stretching back beyond the myths
of ribs and gardens.
And it was mine.
Sometimes I found a doll there
and cleaned it up
and showed it off.
Sometimes the stairs caught fire
and were thickened up with smoke.
But it was always there, my room;
sometimes so quiet,
with trunks and tailors' dummies
like angels, tombstones,
I could hear my heart beat.
And then they said;
'It has to be cleaned out.'
Tears and fear and fury did not soften
their clinical resolve.
Softly they lulled me to sleep.
When I awoke my room was cleared.
I felt like an empty coffin.

ANNE HAVERTY

The Big House

What will they do without their asparagus?
What will they do without calabrese?
Their summer berries minded from the wasps,
Sweet in constant Mayo rain, in shafts
Of sunlight husbanded by the wall.
The roof is fallen into the hall.
No-one anymore looks in catalogues for seed,
Farther than London they've gone, to oblivion.

Not even ghosts can dine on trees.
The roof is fallen into the hall,
The house gapes like the vacant eyes
Of a gassed soldier in the great war.
Down the basement passage to the stables
Where a lad so lately creaked in silks and leather
To run that race that must be and was won,
Drips echo from cracks in the rent stone.
Cook's warm domain stinks like a dungeon.

Brief as the lilac flowers, delicate
As the young pod of a green pea, the vast
Kitchen garden bloomed before the trees,
Cut down, began to grow again. Bounded by the
Wall, raised brick on tawny brick by souls
Potato-fed for luncheon and for breakfast too
To guard the tender leaf and fruit,
An ascendant forest climbs the sky.
The roof is fallen into the hall.

Luminous, ground ivy under the trees,
The air emerald as phosphorous;
Out of the past, a sun is caught
In the ruddy glow of trunks in gloom;
It's weird and meaningless as a dream.
There is no nut nor bud nor plant,
No hoe nor spade disturbs the earth.
Vendettas always reek of death and
These doomy trees avenge Kilcash.
The roof is fallen into the hall.

H. D. (Hilda Doolittle)

Hermetic Definition

There was a Helen before there was a war,
but who remembers her? O grandam, you, you, you,
with faded hair—you answer, you descend,

ascend, from where? it was all over,
I was wrapped in a tight shroud,
but you appear; the death-bands fall away;

you have come, grandam, no toothless grin,
no *corbeau sur une crane*;
'remember,' you say, 'Helen, remember?'

and it is yesterday and the sea wind flutters my veil,
and my brothers stand side by side,
and my sister weaves the blossom for my hair—

laughter? How we laughed together,
I had forgotten—there was always stern command
or fear or loss with the others,

or treachery or guilt or subterfuge;
Odysseus had gone and my sister was to marry
or had married Agamemnon,

and 'this is no great affair,' she confided,
'only laughter, laughter,'
and Menelaus by the altar, whispering

no stinging, honeyed sigh, but
'it's all right it's no great matter,
this will soon be over.'

SEAMUS HEANEY

The Ash Plant

He'll never rise again but he is ready.
Entered like a mirror by the morning,
He stares out the big window, wondering,
Not caring if the day is bright or cloudy.

An upstairs outlook on the whole country.
First milk-lorries, first smoke, cattle, trees
In damp opulence above damp hedges—
He has it to himself, he is like a sentry

Forgotten and unable to remember
The whys and wherefores of his lofty station,
Wakening relieved yet in position,
Disencumbered as a breaking comber.

As his head goes light with light, his wasting hand
Gropes desperately and finds the phantom limb
Of an ash plant in his grasp, which steadies him.
Now he has found his touch he can stand his ground

Or wield the stick like a silver bough and come
Walking again among us: the quoted judge.
I could have cut a better man out of the hedge!
God might have said the same, remembering Adam.

RITA ANN HIGGINS

Anthem

Our fury was well invested
year in, year out.
I wouldn't give an inch,
you wouldn't give an inch.
Hammer and tongs our anthem.

On the morning you died
I could see no reason
to change the habits of a lifetime.

It was strange
saying the rosary round your bed—
half praying, half miming.
The room was cold
with that window open.
Some *piseog* or other was being acted out.
(Letting your spirit dander round Mervue.)

A half-smoked cigarette
lay nipped on your bedside locker,
no *piseog* here only you were probably dying for a drag;
your new fur-lined slippers in everyone's way,
you weren't planning to leave just yet.

The rosary was in full flight—
echoes of the old days
and every bit as long
half song, half whisper,
extra prayers for the devil knows what.

As far as I was concerned
you had died, end of story
end of our Trojan War.

Some nuisance more ancient
than your Conamara lingo
or the jagged stones of Inis Meáin
was playing puck with my sensible side,
the side I use for dancing,

making me for the smallest whisker of a second
want to tuck the blankets round you,
sparing you the waspish November chill.

Ellen Hinsey

On A Visit To Budapest

One cannot live without love—this statement
so simple, so mundane, came to me in that
city where we roamed around the baths. I
hadn't known it until the tilt of your head,
suddenly, in shadow, confirmed all I knew,
and though my children and husband waited
I let you lay me down while the wind berated
the dry leaves overhead. What I hadn't
known was how, at forty, the heart can
reanimate—and how plans, even one's
own flesh, can drift, suddenly out of focus,
seen from the wrong end of a telescope.
When I returned, my husband hadn't noticed.
The children looked up from their play
murmuring their own eccentricities.
I thought about you night and day, until
it seemed I would burst with words unsaid,
unraged. Daylight transfigured all I knew.
Every motion seemed absurd—clothes
packed in trunks seemed like funeral chests
where once I lay down and gave myself away.
I'm not the same as I was at twenty-two,
yet once I was glad to walk the streets
at night and listen to how dawn would light
on my sill. I hear it still, but before today it
was the far-off echo of a voice faded
behind a wall, distance claiming its toll.
If life is hazardous, this the greatest one of all:
the heart cannot be led like a dog
but rises up, and seeks its goal.

PEARSE HUTCHINSON

Benediction

The boy was nearly always bored at Mass
except sometimes at the end
of twelve Mass on a Sunday
when monstrance-blazing, incense-billowing
Benediction raised its golden head
erupting into the church encrusted with
decades of dull stale greasy
shuffling muttering sound,
rescuing that young child
up from his numb trance of boredom onto
a wide-eyed sun-star lunula-glinting
botafumeiro smoky incensual trance of Alive!

You couldn't count on it, mind,
three Sundays often went by bereft of such wild blessing,
but when it did shine forth, for that small boy,
then Benediction
                    was Resurrection
raising him up from the tomb
the long flat Mass had buried him in.

15 Eanáir 1991

D'aimsíos eala
ar chladach thiar,
cnámharlach
craiceann is cleití
ag liobarnaíl sa ghaoith
mar eití fánacha
í triomaithe ag sáile agus sioc,
chomh righin, chomh briosc
go ndéanfainn gaineamh di
de chic.

Bhí a muinéal lúbtha siar
mar bhogha
is íochtar a goib dhuibh
in uachtar
ón bhfreanga deiridh ina cúlfhéith

Riastradh mar sin a tháinig ar Fhionnuala
nuair thit
tonn baiste uirthi
de lámha Phádraig;
cleite is clúmh á dteilgean
ag sean-bhean in arraingeacha báis.

Muinéal mar sin
atá orthu siúd
atá ag feitheamh inniu
le baisteadh ón spéir anuas.

PATRICK KAVANAGH

October

O leafy yellowness you create for me
A world that was and now is poised above time,
I do not need to puzzle out Eternity
As I walk this arboreal street on the edge of a town.
The breeze too, even the temperature
And pattern of movement is precisely the same
As broke my heart for youth passing. Now I am sure
Of something. Something will be mine wherever I am.
I want to throw myself on the public street without caring
For anything but the prayering that the earth offers.
It is October over all my life and the light is staring
As it caught me once in a plantation by the fox coverts.
A man is ploughing ground for winter wheat
And my nineteen years weigh heavily on my feet.

Pounding Rain

News of us spreads like a storm.
The top of our town to the bottom.
We stand behind curtains
parted like hoods; watch each other's eyes.

We talk of moving to the west end,
this bit has always been a shoe box
tied with string; but then again
your father still lives in that house
where we warmed up spaghetti bolognese
in lunch hours and danced to Louis Armstrong,
his gramophone loud as our two heart beats
going boom diddy boom diddy boom.

Did you know then? I started dating Davy;
when I bumped into you I'd just say Hi.
I tucked his photo booth smile into my satchel
brought him out for my pals in the intervals.

A while later I heard you married Trevor Campbell.
Each night I walked into the school dinner hall
stark naked, till I woke to Miss, Miss, Miss Miss
every minute. Then, I bumped into you at the Cross.

You haven't changed you said; that reassurance.
Nor you; your laugh still crosses the street.
I trace you back, beaming, till—
Why don't you come round, Trevor would love it.

He wasn't in. I don't know how it happened.
We didn't bother with a string of do you remembers.
I ran my fingers through the beads in your hair.
Your hair's nice I said stupidly, nice, suits you.

We sat and stared till our eyes filled
like a glass of wine. I did it, the thing
I'd dreamt a million times. I undressed you
slowly, each item of clothing fell
with a sigh. I stroked your silk skin
until we were back in the Campsies, running
down the hills in the pounding rain,
screaming and laughing; soaked right through.

JOHN KEATS

In drear-nighted December

I

In drear-nighted December,
    Too happy, happy tree,
Thy branches ne'er remember
    Their green felicity:
  The north cannot undo them,
  With a sleety whistle through them,
  Nor frozen thawings glue them
    From budding at the prime.

II

In drear-nighted December,
    Too happy, happy brook,
Thy bubblings ne'er remember
    Apollo's summer look;
But with a sweet forgetting,
They stay their crystal fretting,
Never, never petting
    About the frozen time.

III

Ah! would 'twere so with many
    A gentle girl and boy!
But were there ever any
    Writhed not of passèd joy?
  The feel of not to feel it,
  When there is none to heal it,
  Nor numbèd sense to steel it,
    Was never said in rhyme.

D. H. Lawrence

Piano

Softly, in the dusk, a woman is singing to me;
Taking me back down the vista of years, till I see
A child sitting under the piano, in the boom of the tingling strings
And pressing the small, poised feet of a mother who smiles as she
sings.

In spite of myself, the insidious mastery of song
Betrays me back, till the heart of me weeps to belong
To the old Sunday evenings at home, with winter outside
And hymns in the cosy parlour, the tinkling piano our guide.

So now it is vain for the singer to burst into clamour
With the great black piano appassionato. The glamour
Of childish days is upon me, my manhood is cast
Down in the flood of remembrance, I weep like a child for the past.

The Branch

The artist in my father transformed the diagonal
Crack across the mirror on our bathroom cabinet
Into a branch: that was his way of mending things,
A streak of brown paint, dabs of green, an accident
That sprouted leaves,
                        awakening the child in me
To the funny faces he pulls when he is shaving.
He wears a vest, white buttons at his collarbone.
The two halves of my father's face are joining up.
His soapy nostrils disappear among the leaves.

JAMES J. MCAULEY

Landscapes, with Interior

for Paula Cunningham

I Interior

One most beloved, the other our new friend,
Are seated together on the flowered couch:
A Vuillard scene. Their talk is as familiar
And as strange as my aunt and mother murmuring
Before the fire, heads askance in low light,
The mantel with its row of antique jugs,
Spode, Derby, Wedgwood. Fifty years ago
I tried to crack that code of women's talk,
Thinking it would reveal to me the nine
Needs of women I would fulfil as a man.
What kind of fool would attempt to understand?

Ah, friend, you're homesick. I know the welling pain
That follows us from childhood's hearth to the grave.
What should we tell you to sweeten the memories
You took such trouble to pack and carry with you
This far, only to find them troubling your sleep?
You too will make a poetry of this pain,
Draw into your lines the power to change
The leaf, blossom, and bole of Yeats's trope
Into your own code for the heart's troubled seasons.

II Landscapes

Come down the steep trail to a place nearby
Where thermals eddy from the valley floor
Along the layers of the sandy cliff
Into the perfect turquoise bowl of sky.
Martins dive from their little caves
Into clouds of mosquitoes. Warm air rises
To hold the red-tail hawk aloft,
His head sidelong, spying on the rattler
Who spies on the fieldmouse slipping out
To sip from the edge of Hangman Creek.

The heron stoops gray from her gray log
Over the pool where the dappled trout
Is finning upstream through shadowy reeds.
Gold fennel will scatter its sedative tang
Around our heads when we start downstream
Through the tambourine racket of crickets,
So much in tune with the place we forget
This is not ours, 'this huge dome of sky,
This Midas sun. This could never be ours.

A few months more will steal our time.
Winds will blow down the leaves, then snow
Against the house, then Spring, too late
To grow a few bean-rows in time
To bear a crop before summer when we're due
Back on our island, the shock of landfall
After the long flight: the intense green
Under the rushing clouds, the small fields,
The hedges flecked with fuchsia, the gossiping rooks,
The sharp essential odors of grass and sea.

Drink and talk with the family, you
With yours up North, and we, as usual,
Among the glasshouse pleasantries of ours
In the Republic. We'll tell of this hard place,
Its wonders, as if we wouldn't really mind
Returning here to live—although we know
Nothing could make this home. Nothing on earth.

JOAN McBREEN

Girl

A girl in a red skirt
leaps through the bog.
Her bare feet leave
prints on the rocks.

Now she crouches
near a thorn bush,
sheltering from the rain.

And my heart
has kept her all these years
like a stranger.

CATHERINE PHIL MACCARTHY

Birth Mother

That Christmas she asked for photographs.
Without parents.

I checked the last roll
of film developed,
feeling her eyes

smart along a sleeve
all the way to a tiny fist.
That first glimpse, risked

over hot whiskey and cloves
in the quiet of a bar
at closing-time,

silken brown hair
slipping over
an inextricable love,

the wide river of her breath
sparking with red leaves,
intertwined limbs,

her heart breaks all over again
in the white turmoil
of rapids.

Medbh McGuckian

Open Rose

The moon is my second face, her long cycle
Still locked away. I feel rain
Like a tried-on dress, I clutch it
Like a book to my body

His head is there when I work,
It signs my letters with a question-mark;
His hands reach for me like rationed air.
Day by day I let him go

Till I become a woman, or even less,
An incompletely furnished house
That came from a different century
Where I am a guest at my own childhood.

I have grown inside words
Into a state of unbornness,
An open rose on all sides
Has spoken as far as it can.

FRANK McGUINNESS

The Corncrake

for John McCarthy and Brian Keenan

Somewhere in Fermanagh it still survives
In the gentle grass, the corncrake,
Thrashing through the field as happy as Larry,
Its piteous cry its beautiful song.

One summer we were plagued by a corncrake,
Cracking its lullaby—harsh was the night.
Next door 'Pat the Twin' roared in unison,
The whole of Marion Park cursed the bird.

What would I give to hear its song now?
Value what you have, lest it's lost.
Guardians of the air, birds of the earth,
If there be paradise, they live there.

They have seen the world. This solitary cell.
As they fly, in chains, can you hear
The corncrake surviving, singing in Fermanagh,
Remember me, remember me . . .

DEREK MAHON

The Yaddo Letter

(for Rory and Katie)

We are born in an open field and we die in a dark wood.

—Russian proverb

Here among silent lakes and dripping pines
off Route 9P, I write you guys these lines
to ask you what you're up to and what not.
No doubt I'll finish them in my attic flat
in Dublin, if I ever get back there
to the damp gardens of Fitzwilliam Square.
Do you still like your London schools? Do you
still slam the goals in, Rory? Katie-coo,
how goes it with the piano and the flute?
I've a composer in the next-door suite
called Gloria (*in excelsis*), an English novelist,
a sculptor from Vermont, a young ceramist
from Kansas; for we come in suns and snows
from *everywhere* to write, paint and compose.
Sport? We've a pool, closed till the end of May,
a tennis court where no one seems to play;
though there's a horse show, among other things,
starting next week in Saratoga Springs
just down the road—a fascinating place
with spas and concerts and a certain grace . . .
Also a certain measure of renown
since it was here, in an open field north of the town,
that Philip Schuyler clobbered John Burgoyne
in 1777, two hundred and thirteen years ago,
thus helping to precipitate the America we know.
But you're not interested in that kind of stuff;
like me, you'd rather go to the movies for a laugh—
or would you? We talk so infrequently
I hardly know where your real interests lie.
What, for example, are you reading now?
John Buchan? Molly Keane? *Catch-22*?
Nothing too highbrow, time enough for that;

you're better off with a flute or a cricket bat.
You're only (only!) in your middle teens,
too young to be thinking about *seerious* things
like the dream plays and ghost sonatas your
lost father hears and watches everywhere,
especially when he glimpses happy families
a-picnicking among the squirrel trees.
I try to imagine you asleep, at work,
or walking with your mother in Hyde Park
where once we walked each Sunday, hand in hand,
to feed the daffy ducks on the Round Pond,
chucking crumbs to the ones we liked the best,
comical, tufted yellow-eyes, ignoring all the rest.
Remember birthday parties, rockets at Hallowe'en,
bus-rides to Covent Garden to see Eugene?
The day we drove to Brighton? Maybe not.
Summer and winter I would rise and trot
my fingers up your backs like a mad mouse
to wake you chuckling. Now I wake in a silent house
in a dark wood. Once, 'Is it morning time?',
asked Katie waking. Now it is mourning time
in a black heart; but I will not forget
the nooks and corners of our crazy flat,
its dormer windows and its winding stair,
gulls on the roof, its views of *everywhere*!
When Mummy and I split up and I lived in Co. Cork
among the yacht crowd and bohemian folk
I'd wander round the hills above Kinsale
where English forces clobbered Hugh O'Neill
in Tudor times, wrecking the Gaelic order
(result, plantations and the present Border),
or dander down along the Bandon River
wondering when next we'd be together;
then home to a stable loft where I could hear
mysterious night sounds whispering in my ear—
wood-pigeons, foxes, silence, my own brain,
my lamp a lighthouse in the drizzling rain.
After a month of fog a day would dawn
when the rain ceased, cloud cleared and the sun shone;
then magical white wisps of smoke would rise
and I'd think of our own magical London years.
'One always loses with a desperate throw.'

What I lost was a wife, a life, and you.
As for love, a treasure when first it's new,
it all too often fades away, for both, like the morning dew;
yet it remains the one sure thing to cling to
as I cling like grim death to the thought of you,
sitting alone here in upstate New York,
half-way to Montreal, trying to work,
lit by Tiffany lamps, Sinéad O'Connor on the stereo.
This above all, to thine own selves be true,
remembering seaside games in stormy Ulster parts
and Sunday lunches at the Chelsea Arts
with lemonade for you in paper cups,
snooker and candlelight for the 'grown-ups'.
Your father (yawn!) has seen enough mischance
trying to figure out the dancers from the dance.
Like Mummy, *some* can dance; I never could,
no more than I could ever see the birches for the wood.
We are *all* children; and when either of you
feels scared or miserable, as you must sometimes do,
look to us, but remember we do too.
I hear the big trucks flashing through the night
like Christmas road-houses ablaze with light,
symbols of modern movement and romance;
but the important thing is permanence—
for you, a continuity with the past
enabling you to prosper, and a fast
forward to where the paradoxes grow
like crocuses in our residual snow;
for me, a long devotion to the art
in which you play such an important part,
a long devotion to the difficult Muse
your mother was, despite our difficulties.
Everything thrives in contrariety—no
thesis without antithesis (and synthesis?); no black
without its white, like a hot sun on the ice of a Yaddo lake.
Children of light, may your researches be
reflections on this old anomaly;
may you remember, as the years go by
and you grow slowly towards maturity,
that life consists in the receipt of life,
its fun and games, its boredom and its grief;
that no one, sons or daughters, fathers, wives,

escapes the rough stuff that makes up our lives.
Equip yourselves in every way you can
to take it like a woman or a man,
respecting values you've long understood
pertaining to the true, the beautiful and the good.
Sorry to sound so tedious and trite.
I'd hoped to be more fun and try to write
you something entertaining as I often try to do;
but this time round I wanted to be *seerious* and true
to felt experience. My love 2U.
Nothing I say you don't already know.
Football and flute, you'll join us soon enough
in the mad 'grown-up' world of Henry James's 'stupid life'.
Write soon and tell me all about your work.
It's time now for your father to be heading for New York,
a city worse than London, rife with confrontation,
much like the one you see on television.
Maybe I'll read this letter at the 'Y'
and tell you all about it by and by.
I hope I haven't bored you stiff already.
Write to me soon in Dublin.

My love, as ever,

—Daddy.

JOSÉ MARTÍ

Little Horseman

Translated by Louise C. Callaghan

In the morning
my little fellow
woke me
with kisses.

Astride
my chest,
he'd grip my hair
for reins.

Wild with pleasure,
I wild the same
spur me on—
my little horseman:

What sweet spurs
his chilly feet!
How he laughed,
my little rider!

And I used to kiss
those two little feet,
so small, they fit
into one kiss!

AIDAN MATHEWS

Thee

Weddings first and then christenings and then funerals.
It's as straightforward as subject, verb, object,
This move from the altar to the font to the mortuary chapel.
How it leaves us speechless, how it takes our breath away!
Yet the day I helped to carry my brother's coffin
There was the sound of confetti under my desert boots,
And after the worst two years since our records began,
The cot has come out of our attic like a Jew after a pogrom.
Amid all the bloodshed, we are one flesh assuming it,
At a standstill certainly, uncertainly, but still standing.

At the time of writing, the garden is dead and buried.
But come whenever, Passover say, or at Pentecost,
The kids will be playing Mass with their chocolate buttons,
Inventing miracle stories out of the telephone book
Where the ivy has gone and greened the cable for Cable TV
And the blackbird returns to her nest with a drinking straw from a
    Coke;
And I will be there, observing their serving, giving thanks
For our dying days in the land of the living; thanksgiving
For this indefinite time, this world, this definite article
Pronounced like the ancient form of a pronoun that stands for
    you.

CAITLÍN MAUDE

Aimhréidhe

Siúil, a ghrá,
Cois trá anocht—
Siúil agus cuir uait
na deora—
éirigh agus siúil anocht

ná feac do ghlúin feasta
ag uaigh sin an tsléibhe—
tá na blátha sin feoite
agus tá mo chnámhasa dreoite . . .

(Labhraim leat anocht
ó íochtar mara—
labhraim leat gach oíche
ó íochtar mara . . .)

Shiúileas lá cois trá
shiúileas go híochtar trá—
rinne tonn súgradh le tonn—
ligh an cúr bán mo chosa—
d'ardaíos mo shúil go mall
gur ansiúd amuigh ar an domhain
in aimhréidhe cúir agus toinn
chonaic an t-uaigneas id shúil
'gus an doilíos id ghnúis

Shiúileas amach ar an domhain
ó ghlúine go com
agus ó chom go guaillí
nó gur slogadh mé
sa doilíos 'gus san uaigneas

CAITLÍN MAUDE

Entangled

Translated by Celia de Fréine

Walk along the strand
tonight, my love,
step out and stop
your keening
stir yourself and walk abroad

kneel no more
at that mountain grave—
those flowers have wilted,
my bones decayed . . .

(I speak to you tonight
from the seabed—
I speak to you each night
from the seabed . . .)

Once I walked along the strand
down to the water's edge—
wave romped with wave—
white foam licked my feet—
I lifted my eyes slowly
and out there in the deep
woven among wave and foam
I saw the loneliness in your eye,
the grief on your face

I trod into the deep
from knee to waist,
waist to shoulder
until I was engulfed
by grief and desolation

Medicine

for Anthony

Dream of a tiger
or a standing bear
is big medicine.
We've had our own
in the field-mice and bees
and the lighting glimpse of a hare
in the covert of the legendary fox.

We've played in our dreams' demesne,
stood by the fairy fort
invisibly joining hands.
I've watched you when you didn't know,
to send mothering out like she would;
you've calmed my nerves
with kinder truths and disprin.
Yes, you've helped my pain.

And if the glaring yellow lines
of man-done time
should come breaking things in parts
we can swallow this capsule
and sink safe—
into the christmas mornings
and the nights of booze
and the songs we sang anyway
and saturday afternoons in O'Neills'
and the certainty that the place still holds
where we were home.

PAULA MEEHAN

for Kay Foran

The Exact Moment I Became A Poet

was in 1963 when Miss Shannon
rapping her duster on the easel's peg
half obscured by a cloud of chalk

said *Attend to your books, girls,*
or mark my words, you'll end up
in the sewing factory.

It wasn't just that some of the girls'
mothers worked in the sewing factory
or even that my own aunt did,

and many neighbours, but
that those words 'end up' robbed
the labour of its dignity.

Not that I knew it then,
not in those words—labour, dignity.
That's all back construction,

making sense; allowing also
the teacher was right
and no one knows it like I do myself.

But: I *saw* them: mothers, aunts and neighbours
trussed like chickens
on a conveyor belt,

getting sewn up the way my granny
sewed the sage and onion stuffing
in the birds.

Words could pluck you,
leave you naked,
your lovely, shiny feathers all gone.

ÁINE MILLER

In the Garden at Barna

The present is pushy, full of itself.

Marigolds bat their lashes at me,
grasses are frantically waving.
The bog deal elbows the hydrangea,
griselinias call attention to themselves
by constant fidget.
Anything to catch my eye.

   Beyond, the sea, sudsy, busy,
   gathers and launders the sky's greys,
   carrying on. Gulls
   dazzle to a white horizon.

Across the Bay, Clare, harbours the inward.
The mind's rays light it in
and out of focus. Memories
gloom behind a shower.
The break when it comes is radiance.

   Now sees some shift,
   that hedge, those firs, wall, my bulk,
   budge up.

The past is on the move again.

NOEL MONAHAN

In School

We remembered and forgot,
We repeated, remembered and forgot,
We recited and forgot,
We chalked on slates,
We rubbed it out.
We did sums with pencils.
We dipped into inkwells,
We made letters with pen and ink,
    small letters between blue lines
      BIG LETTERS BETWEEN RED LINES.
We crossed out words,
We crossed out lines.
We soaked up blobs
    on pink blotting paper.

The school added us.
The school subtracted us.
The school multiplied us.
The school divided us.

JOHN MONTAGUE

Within

To open a door
and step into
a magic garden.
Childhood dreams
of it, somewhere
a gate hinge among

the tall flowers,
tangled creepers,
or a small knob
lost under petals.
No one watches as
you slowly push

the secret entrance
open, to escape from
those everlasting calls
of *Where are you?*
Come back home
at once, please!

Orders, injunctions,
you will not hear
beyond that door
safe in the silence,
brushed by the hover-
ing wings of butterflies,

the same warm beauty
as on the outside, all
colour and movement,
leaves shifting, sighing,
a branch trembling
as though near speech.

The air rinsed clear,
bright with potency,
as if some magic figure—
a stooped gardener,
or a friendly giant—
might suddenly appear,

but only the self
listening to the self,
awash with stillness,
taut with anticipation,
bright with awareness,
far from the botheration.

ÁGNES NEMES NAGY

The Sleeping Form

Translated by Hugh Maxton

Unknown and naked,
you rise from ash.
You are in the seventh room,
not dead, only sleeping.

Only sleeping, bed of whittles,
between the ashen walls,
the wrecked curtain gives the silence
huge motionless wings.

I do not move.
Only, like slowly tumbling sheaves
only your visions in their courses
move, like black stars.

Wake, wake up. Uncover that shoulder.
Wounded or not. I will find you.
Talk that I may talk till death.
Speak, speak finally wherever
in your mute dream.

PABLO NERUDA

Memory

Translated by Alastair Reid

I have to remember everything,
keep track of blades of grass, the threads
of the untidy event, and
the houses, inch by inch,
the long lines of the railway,
the textured face of pain.

If I should get one rosebush wrong
and confuse night with a hare,
or even if one whole wall
has crumbled in my memory,
I have to make the air again,
steam, the earth, leaves,
hair and bricks as well,
the thorns which pierced me,
the speed of the escape.

Take pity on the poet.

I was always quick to forget
and in those hands of mine
grasped only the intangible
and unrelated things,
which could only be compared
by being non-existent.

The smoke was like an aroma,
the aroma was like smoke,
the skin of a sleeping body
which woke to my kisses;
but do not ask me the date
or the name of what I dreamed—
I cannot measure the road
which may have had no country,
or that truth which changed,
which the day perhaps subdued
to become a wandering light
like a firefly in the dark.

EILÉAN NÍ CHUILLEANÁIN

The House Remembered

The house persists, the permanent
Scaffolding while the stones move round.
Convolvulus winds the bannisters, sucks them down;
We found an icicle under the stairs
Tall as a church candle;
It refused to answer questions
But proved its point by freezing hard.

The house changes, the stones
Choking in dry lichen stupidly spreading
Abusing the doorposts, frost on the glass.
Nothing stays still, the house is still the same
But the breast over the sink turned into a tap
And coming through the door all fathers look the same.

The stairs and windows waver but the house stands up;
Peeling away the walls another set shows through.
I can't remember, it happened too recently.
But somebody was born in every room.

Nuala Ní Dhomhnaill

Scéala

Do chuimhnigh sí
go deireadh thiar
ar scáil an aingil
sa teampall,
cleitearnach sciathán
ina timpeall;
is dúiseacht le dord colúr
is stealladh ga gréine
ar fhallaí aolcloch
an lá a fuair sí an scéala.

É siúd
d'imigh
is n'fheadar ar chuimhnigh riamh
ar cad a d'eascair
óna cheathrúna,
dhá mhíle bliain
d'iompar croise
de dhóiteán is deatach,
de chlampar chomh hard
le spící na Vatacáine.

Ó, a mhaighdean rócheansa,
nár chuala trácht ar éinne riamh
ag teacht chughat sa doircheacht
cosnocht, déadgheal
is a shúile lán de rógaireacht.

NUALA NÍ DHOMHNAILL

Annunciations

Translated by Michael Hartnett

She remembered to the very end
the angelic vision
in the temple:
the flutter of wings
about her—
noting the noise of doves,
sun-rays raining
on lime-white walls—
the day she got the tidings.

He—
he went away
and perhaps forgot
what grew in his loins—
two thousand years
of carrying a cross
two thousand years
of smoke and fire
of rows that reached a greater span
than the spires of the Vatican.

Remember
o most tender virgin Mary
that never was it known
that a man came to you
in the darkness alone,
his feet bare, his teeth white
and roguery swelling in his eyes.

JULIE O'CALLAGHAN

Sipper Lids

It didn't feel so hot
when I found out about
those sipper lids.
We were driving to hardware stores
like it was the good old days.
The air was July
and the sun was too.
'Don't put the brownies
on the dashboard—they'll melt.'
I'm pulling off the lid
on my honey-sweetened coffee,
when my dad tells me not to.
'Watch me'—he picks up his coffee,
puts the lid to his mouth.
(He's doing this and steering.)
As I look over at him
sipping from the little gashes
in the plastic lid,
I know all is lost.
I might as well have been
the older kid from Italy
stuck at the back
of our Chicago classroom
because she didn't speak English.
Some kind of foreigner
who never heard of sipper lids.

Volpi

He should have been an Italian tenor, belting out the high ones
in Carnegie and adoring the applause, the rattle of their jewellery
instead of pencil-cases, rulers as we fidgeted in class, half-listening
while he interrupted the conjugation of a difficult French verb
and swished his gown back like a curtain to show us all
another excerpt from the movie of his life. Such glamour
and such danger: how he'd stood out on the wing of a plane
at thirty thousand feet or climbed into the mouth of a volcano
so as to pluck a fallen infant from the boiling lava. And never
Sir or Mister; always, always *Signor* Volpi, which he explained
was close to vulpine, fox-like (though he was naturally a direct
descendant of the wolf-cub who built Rome). His once-great brush
long gone; just a couple of grey strands held in place with hair-oil.
Smirking we laid traps for him, alarm clocks going off in cupboards,
the duster studded with match-heads lighting like a flare in his hand
as he tried to wipe the blackboard clean. The more we disbelieved
the more the stories grew: we shivered in our singlets at Gymnastics,
sniggering as he taught us how to march like Mussolini. Slowly we
closed in, his face purpling with shock when the banger went off at the back;
outright laughter as he recalled his role in the Charge of the Light Brigade,
and not forgetting of course the time his back was turned when we
heaved every desk right up to where he stood, surrounding him. And his
high-pitched scream. And how, when he came back to say goodbye
three months later, having been 'out sick' he hobbled on a little cane,
one foot dragging loose where the teeth of the snare had been.

DENNIS O'DRISCOLL

Deadlines

The suspense of hanging
  around for an arbitrary call,
passing the years until

you're summoned, pacing
  between walls without
a firm appointment:

Read a glossy magazine.
  Break the crossword code.
Sit it out in your office,

driven to distraction
  by the workload;
at home, restore the paint

a malicious nail has
  scarred your car with;
threaten lawyers' letters

on your noisy neighbours;
  study the small print
in the share prospectus.

Your time will come
  when it gets a minute,
refusing to be pinned down,

despatching you at whim
  with a mercifully sudden
heart attack, snapping your back

in a car accident, setting
  your nightwear alight
in a hotel inferno,

taking your memory away
  so that you can't quite
put a name on its blank face.

SHEILA O'HAGAN

The Wood Pigeon

A tree bends over you like Yeats' old thorn,
How desolate the day, your place in it.
I push the graveyard gate, walk slowly through
The gloomy avenues of fern and stone.
I buried you in the wrong place, the wind
Is softer from the west than from the east,
Your feet should face the sea like any Celt.
But I'll do what I can to clear your space,
Brush off the sodden leaves, replace the lead
Of letters fallen off your name, our name.
And I'll not ask what of you perished first
Yet hear the truth, that all is gathered up
In human love. I've left you some flowers.
Is it the rain or you who flays my face,
Or wind dements my hair? I turn to leave,
A wood pigeon breaks from the trees, a whirr
Soft as a ghost. I listen to it
As it comes and goes, comes and goes.

CAITRÍONA O'REILLY

Nineteen Eighty-Four

Saint Laurence O'Toole meant business
with his high cheekbones and stiff mitre.
Mary wore lipstick and no shoes
so I sat on her side of the altar.

She wasn't frightening at all
as with her halo at a rakish angle,
she trod on plaster clouds and stars
behind a row of five pence candles.

She always appeared ignorant
of her swelling middle, or
even politely averted her eyes
(and she never got any bigger).

Later on I couldn't look
for fear she might suddenly move.
That year whole crowds of Marys
wept bloody tears in their groves,

making signs with fragmented hands.
And I knew or guessed why—
the worst thing a schoolgirl could do
was to give birth alone and die

under Mary's hapless supervision.
No apparitions in grottoes
or winged babies with cradle-cap
for the likes of those.

Do Jack Kerouac

do Shéamas de Bláca

'The only people for me are the mad ones,
the ones who are mad to live, mad to talk,
mad to be saved, desirous of everything at
the same time, the ones who never yawn or
say a commonplace thing but burn,
burn like fabulous yellow roman candles'
Sliocht as *On the Road*

Ag sioscadh trí do shaothar anocht tháinig leoithne na cuimhne
chugam ó gach leathanach.

Athmhúsclaíodh m'óige is mhothaigh mé ag éirí ionam an *beat*
brionglóideach a bhí ag déanamh aithris ort i dtús na seachtóidí.

1973. Bhí mé *hookáilte* ort. Lá i ndiaidh lae fuair mé *shot* inspioráide
ó do shaothar a ghealaigh m'aigne is a shín mo shamhlaíocht.

Ní Mín 'a Leá ná Fána Bhuí a bhí á fheiceáil agam an t-am adaí ach
machairí Nebraska agus táilte féaraigh Iowa.

Agus nuair a thagadh na *bliúanna* orm ní bealach na Bealtaine a bhí
romham amach ach mórbhealach de chuid Mheiriceá.

'Hey man you gotta stay high,' a déarfainn le mo chara agus muid
ag *freakáil* trí Chailifornia Chill Ulta isteach go Frisco an Fháil
Charraigh.

Tá do leabhar ina luí druidte ar m'ucht ach faoi chraiceann an
chlúdaigh tá do chroí ag preabadaigh i bhféitheog gach focail.

Oh man mothaím arís, na *higheanna* adaí ar Himiléithe na hóige:

Ó chósta go cósta thriall muid le chéile, saonta, spleodrach,
místiúrtha;

Oilithreacht ordóige ó Nua-Eabhrac go Frisco agus as sin go Cathair
Mheicsiceo;

Beat buile inár mbeatha. Spreagtha. Ag bladhmadh síos bóithre i
gCadillacs ghasta ag sciorradh thar íor na céille ar eiteoga na
m*bennies*.

Thrasnaigh muid teorainneacha agus thrasnaigh muid taibhrithe.

Cheiliúraigh muid gach casadh ar bhealach ár mbeatha, *binge*anna
agus bráithreachas ó Bhrooklyn go Berkeley, *booze, bop* agus
Búdachas; Éigse na hÁise; sreangscéalta as an tsíoraíocht ar na

Sierras; marijuana agus misteachas i Meicsiceo; brionglóidi buile i mBixby Canyon.

Rinne muid Oirféas as gach *orifice*.

Ó is cuimhneach liom é go léir, a Jack, an chaint is an cuartú.
Ba tusa bard beoshúileach na mbóithre, ar thóir na foirfeachta, ar thóir na bhFlaitheas.
Is cé nach bhfuil aon aicearra chuig na Déithe, adeirtear, d'éirigh leatsa slí a aimsiú in amantaí nuair a d'fheistigh tú úim adhainte ar Niagara d'aigne le *dope* is le diagacht.
Is i mBomaite sin na Buile gineadh solas a thug spléachadh duit ar an tSíoraíocht,
Is a threoraigh 'na bhaile tú, ta súil agam, lá do bháis chuig Whitman, Proust, agus Rimbaud.

Tá mo bhealach féin romham amach . . . *'a road that ah zigzags all over creation. Yeah man! Ain't nowhere else it can go. Right!'*
Agus lá inteacht ar bhealach na seanaoise is na scoilteacha
Nó lá níos cóngaraí do bhaile, b'fhéidir,
Scriocfidh mé Crosbhealach na Cinniúna is beidh an Bás romham ansin,
Treoraí tíriúil le mé a thabhairt thar teorainn,
Is ansin, *goddammit* a Jack, beidh muid beirt ag síobshiúl sa tSíoraíocht.

CATHAL Ó SEARCAIGH

To Jack Kerouac

For Séamus de Bláca

Translated by Sara Berkeley

'The only people for me are the mad ones,
the ones who are mad to live, mad to talk,
mad to be saved, desirous of everything at
the same time, the ones who never yawn or
say a commonplace thing but burn, burn like
fabulous yellow roman candles'
                    On the Road

Thumbing through your work tonight the aroma of memories came
   from every page.
My youth rewoke and I felt rising in me the dreamy beat that imitated
   you at the start of the '70s.
1973. I was hooked on you. Day after day I got shots of inspiritation
   from your life which lit my mind and stretched my imagination.
I didn't see Mín 'a Leá or Fána Bhuí then, but the plains of Nebraska
   and the grassy lands of Iowa
And when the blues came it wasn't the Bealtaine road that beckoned
   but a way stretching across America.
'Hey man you gotta stay high,' I'd say to my friend as we freaked
   through California's Cill Ulta into Frisco's Falcarragh.

Your book lies shut on my breast, your heart beating under the skin
   cover in the muscle of every word.
Oh man I feel them again, those highs on youth's Himalayas from
   coast to coast we roamed together, free, wild, reckless:
A hitchhiking odyssey from New York to Frisco and down to Mexico
   City.
A mad beat to our lives. Crazed. Hurtling down highways in speeding
   cars, skidding over the verge of sanity on the wings of Benzedrine.
We crossed frontiers and we scaled dreams.
Celebrations at every turn of life's highway, binges and brotherhood

from Brooklyn to Berkeley; booze, bop and Buddhism; Asian verse;
   telegrams from a Sierra eternity; marijuana and mysticism in
   Mexico; frenzied visions in Bixby Canyon.

Orpheus emerged from every orifice.

O I remember it all Jack, the talk and the quest.
You were the wild-eyed poet walking free, searching for harmony,
   searching for Heaven.
And although it is said there is no shortcut to the Gods you
   opened one up now and then, harnessing your mind's Niagara
   with dope and divinity.
And in those rapturous moments you generated the light that you
   saw eternity by
And that guided you, I hope, the day of your death, home to
   Whitman, Proust, and Rimbaud.

My road is before me 'a road that ah zigzags all over creation.
   Yeah man! Ain't nowhere else it can go. Right!'
And someday, on the road of failing sight and knotted limbs
Or a less distant day, perhaps
Death will face me at Fate's Crossroads
My gentle companion across the frontier
And then, goddamit Jack, we'll both be hiking across eternity.

Death of a Season

Translated by Catherine O'Brien

All night long it rained
on the memories of summer.

We went out in the dark
between the dismal thundering of stones,
standing on the brink with outstretched lanterns
to explore the danger of the bridges.

Pale at dawn we saw the swallows
drenched and motionless on the wires
looking out for secret signals to depart—

and on the ground they were reflected
in the defeated faces of the fountains.

MINNIE BRUCE PRATT

Done

When you're gone out of town, the way I get you back is
I masturbate. If you're away this week, next week, no matter.
I raise one hand. In a second it's your tongue on my clitoris,
your head's weight on my lap in the striped pink armchair,
your jaw opening like a thought between my thighs, lower,
your tongue a delicate knifeblade licking stone. My wetness
eases your work. My blood satisfies the heat with a tremor.
You lift your head. Done, my hands lift.
Under my ass there is a cold damp like saliva. Nothing else left.

Back, at 2 a.m., you're more than the sharp memory I angled
between my legs, sensation after the day's numb headlines.
Your hand sweats and dreams on my stomach, not your imagined
hand in my jeans in the backyard dark, no clandestine
act while above us a neighbor's cigarette shines red.
In the garden a moonflower is stretching its jaws in the cold,
its smell of my mother's face powder, its skin like your skin.
I drowse. Everything outside this room is alone.
I move. You say my name. Your hip backs me like warm stone.

ADRIENNE RICH

For Memory

Old words: *trust   fidelity*
Nothing new yet to take their place.

I rake leaves, clear the lawn, October grass
painfully green beneath the gold
and in this silent labor thoughts of you
start up
I hear your voice: *disloyalty   betrayal*
stinging the wires

I stuff the old leaves into sacks
and still they fall and still
I see my work undone

One shivering rainswept afternoon
and the whole job to be done over

I can't know what you know
unless you tell me
there are gashes in our understandings
of this world
We came together in a common
fury of direction
barely mentioning difference
(what drew our finest hairs
to fire
the deep, difficult troughs
unvoiced)
I fell through a basement railing
the first day of school and cut my forehead open—
did I ever tell you? More than forty years
and I still remember smelling my own blood
like the smell of a new schoolbook

And did you ever tell me
how your mother called you in from play
and from whom? To what? These atoms filmed by
    ordinary dust
that common life we each and all bent out of orbit from
to which we must return simply to say
this is where I came from
this is what I knew

The past is not a husk   yet change goes on

Freedom. It isn't once, to walk out
under the Milky Way, feeling the rivers
of light, the fields of dark—
freedom is daily, prose-bound, routine
remembering. Putting together, inch by inch
the starry worlds. From all the lost collections.

Childhood

Translated by J. B. Leishman

The school's long stream of time and tediousness
winds slowly on, through torpor, through dismay.
O loneliness, O time that creeps away . . .
Then out at last: the streets ring loud and gay,
and in the big white squares the fountains play,
and in the parks the world seems measureless.—
And to pass through it all in children's dress,
with others, but quite otherwise than they:—
O wondrous time, O time that fleets away,
O loneliness!

And out into it all to gaze and gaze:
men, women, women, men in blacks and greys,
and children, brightly dressed, but differently;
and here a house, and there a dog, maybe,
and fear and trust changing in subtle ways:—
O grief uncaused, O dream, O dark amaze.
O still-unsounded sea!

And then with bat and ball and hoop to playing
in parks where bright colours softly fade,
brushing against the grown-ups without staying
when ball or hoop their alien walks invade;
but when the dwilight comes, with little, swaying
footsteps going home with unrejected aid:—
O thoughts that fade into the darkness, straying
alone, afraid!

And hours on end by the grey pond-side kneeling
with little sailing-boat and elbows bare;
forgetting it, because one like it's stealing
below the ripples, but with sails more fair;
and, having still to spare, to share some feeling
with the small sinking face caught sight of there:—
Childhood! Winged likenesses half-guessed at, wheeling,
oh, where, oh, where?

CHRISTINA ROSSETTI

Song

When I am dead, my dearest,
  Sing no sad song for me;
Plant thou no roses at my head,
  Nor shady cypress tree:
Be the green grass above me
  With showers and dewdrops wet;
And if thou wilt, remember,
  And if thou wilt, forget.

I shall not see the shadows,
  I shall not feel the rain;
I shall not hear the nightingale
  Sing on as if in pain:
And dreaming through the twilight
  That doth not rise nor set,
Haply I may remember,
  And haply may forget.

NELLY SACHS

If I Only Knew

Translated by Ruth & Matthew Mead

If I only knew
On what your last look rested.
Was it a stone that had drunk
So many last looks that they fell
Blindly upon its blindness?

Or was it earth,
Enough to fill a shoe,
And black already
With so much parting
And with so much killing?

Or was it your last road
That brought you a farewell from all the roads
You had walked?

A puddle, a bit of shining metal,
Perhaps the buckle of your enemy's belt,
Or some other small augury
Of heaven?

Or did this earth,
Which lets no one depart unloved,
Send you a bird-sign through the air,
Reminding your soul that it quivered
In the torment of its burnt body?

WILLIAM SHAKESPEARE

When that I was and a little tiny boy

from *Twelfth Night, or What You Will*

When that I was and a little tiny boy,
    With hey, ho, the wind and the rain,
A foolish thing was but a toy,
    For the rain it raineth every day.

But when I came to man's estate,
    With hey, ho, the wind and the rain,
'Gainst knaves and thieves men shut their gate,
    For the rain it raineth every day.

But when I came, alas! to wive,
    With hey, ho, the wind and the rain,
By swaggering could I never thrive,
    For the rain it raineth every day.

But when I came unto my beds,
    With hey, ho, the wind and the rain,
With toss-pots still had drunken heads,
    For the rain it raineth every day.

A great while ago the world begun,
    With hey, ho, the wind and the rain,
But that's all one, our play is done,
    And we'll strive to please you every day.

CHARLES SIMIC

Gray-Headed Schoolchildren

Old men have bad dreams,
So they sleep little.
They walk on bare feet
Without turning on the lights,
Or they stand leaning
On gloomy furniture
Listening to their hearts beat.

The one window across the room
Is black like a blackboard.
Every old man is alone
In this classroom, squinting
At that fine chalk line
That divides being-here
From being-here-no-more.

No matter. It was a glass of water
They were going to get,
But not just yet.
They listen for mice in the walls,
A car passing on the street,
Their dead fathers shuffling past them
On their way to the kitchen.

Expulsion. A Foetal Hymn

How terrible it is to be expelled
out of the womb
I was saddened from then on
like I knew no one
and no one knew me
like I felt desolate
you see in there things
were orchestrated differently.

My mother loved my coming
I'd hear her sing bubble music
beautiful
to be so alone inside her
my head its own shape
question shape
my ears still growing
my mouth never open
my lips like cherry blossoms
and my eyes the eyes of heart
of seeing nothing but stars
no not stars
other biochemical things.

I swam and swam
and my Mam loved me
not because I loved her
how would she know anyway
but 'cause I made her feel fine
like a woman should feel—
curled shape at night
to remind me no mother Mam
no one round to love me.

I terrible fright to be expelled
like being thrown out
nothing special about me
no womb to cover over protect
every creature has her skin
and I had mine—it's gone
you see me I'm naked
a stupid sheep sheared naked
yearning massive creature
cold on the hill
lost in fog
no mother Mam
my skin over her memory.

To be back there sometime
like dying like saying
'Why Mam when I loved you
you threw me out and now
I've spent all time
no time searching.'
To be back like your mouth
birthed me
and I'm crawling in again
dying to love you
and you to love me
and we belong
beloved of each other—
never again mother
Mam gone
and me alone knowing no one
and no one knowing me.

GARY SNYDER

Ripples on the Surface

'Ripples on the surface of the water—
were silver salmon passing under—different
from the ripples caused by breezes'

A scudding plume on the wave—
a humpback whale is
breaking out in air up
gulping herring
          —Nature not a book, but a *performance*, a
high old culture

Ever-fresh events
scraped out, rubbed out, and used, used again—
the braided channels of the rivers
hidden under fields of grass—

The vast wild
          the house, alone.
The little house in the wild,
          the wild in the house.
Both forgotten.

No nature

Both together, one big empty house.

Triumph of being . . .

Translated by David McDuff

What have I to fear? I am a part of infinity.
I am a part of the all's great power,
a lonely world inside millions of worlds,
like a star of the first degree that fades last.
Triumph of living, triumph of breathing, triumph of being!
Triumph of feeling time run ice-cold through one's veins
and of hearing the silent river of the night
and of standing on the mountain under the sun.
I walk on sun, I stand on sun,
I know of nothing else than sun.

Time—convertress, time—destructress, time—enchantress,
do you come with new schemes, a thousand tricks to offer me
    existence
as a little seed, as a coiled snake, as a rock amidst the sea?
Time—you murderess—leave me!
The sun fills my breast with sweet honey up to the brim
and she says: all stars fade at last, but they always shine without
    fear.

ANNE STEVENSON

Leaving

Habits the hands have, reaching for this and that,
   (tea kettle, orange squeezer, milk jug,
   frying pan, sugar jar, coffee mug)
manipulate, or make, a habitat,
become its *genii loci*, working on
quietly in the kitchen when you've gone.

Objects a house keeps safe on hooks and shelves
   (climbing boots, garden tools, backpacks
   bird feeders, tennis balls, anoraks)
the day you leave them bleakly to themselves,
do they decide how long, behind the door,
to keep your personality in store?

Good Bishop Berkeley made the objects stay
just where we leave them when we go away
by lending them to God. If so, God's mind
is crammed with things abandoned by mankind
   (featherbeds, chamber pots, flint lighters,
   quill pens, sealing wax, typewriters),

an archive of the infinitely there.
But there for whom? For what museum? And where?
I like to think of spiders, moths, white worms
leading their natural lives in empty rooms
   (egg-sacks, mouse-litter, dead flies,
   cobwebs, silverfish, small eyes)

while my possessions cease to study me
   (*Emma, The Signet Shakespeare, Saving Whales.
   Living with Mushrooms, Leviathan, Wild Wales*).
Habit by habit, they sink through time to be
one with the mind or instinct of the place,
home in its shadowy silence and stone space.

Welcome

I have killed countless times.

Killing is too easy.
Dying also.
Living is hard.

At a young age, eight or so,
I castrated a man, a baddie,
sketched execrably
in my brother's cowboy magazine.
I spent a heated hour or thereabouts
doing this, one Saturday morning.
My brother was with my parents:
they had taken him town-shopping
in the pony trap, leaving me.

I, fighting to be favourite,
jeopardised all possibility,
contradicted—serious offence—
answered back—another, was called
brazen hussy. Our parents worked
and worked. Once, I sobbed out grief
to the girl—no-one ever said *maid*—
that was for townee snobs
with daughters in lahdedah convents.

The girl did her best,
my parents working
and working,
but I believed myself
unfavoured;
I unwished that self,
wanting to be
as he,
my brother.

The district liked him,
he made it laugh:
he had male scope.
The people prized
his wish to stay;
they took
his lack of push
for loyalty to roots.
He was theirs.

For years
he pushed me down
with fists, feet, words—
no lack there.
I longed for him:
Please like me, my brother.
I never said it.
Instead, I began to make
advantage from my difference.

Hungry, urgent, I outdistanced him,
ate new territory, proved
some femaleship. All so long ago.
Somewhere in the years, he inscribed
a book to me: *With love*. Solitary
declaration. I had won.
But by that time
I knew all his fears:
it was no victory.

Now, there are so many dead.
I am tired of competitions,
spend much time with hindsight.
Anyone may visit me.

WISLAWA SZYMBORSKA

Memory At Last

Translated by Magnus J. Krynski & Robert A. Morgan

Memory at last has what it sought.
My mother has been found, my father glimpsed.
I dreamed up for them a table, two chairs. They sat down.
Once more they seemed close, and once more living for me.
With the lamps of their two faces, at twilight,
they suddenly gleamed as if for Rembrandt.

Only now can I relate
the many dreams in which they've wandered, the many throngs
in which I've pulled them out from under wheels,
the many death-throes where they have collapsed into my arms.
Cut off—they would grow back crooked.
Absurdity forced them into masquerade.
Small matter that this could not hurt them outside me
if it hurt them inside me.
The gawking rabble of my dreams heard me calling 'mamma'
to something that hopped squealing on a branch.
And they laughed because I had a father with a ribbon in his hair.
I would wake up in shame.

Well, at long last.
On a certain ordinary night,
between a humdrum Friday and Saturday,
they suddenly appeared exactly as I wished them.
Seen in a dream, they yet seemed freed from dreams,
obedient only to themselves and nothing else.
All possibilities vanished from the background of the image,
accidents lacked a finished form.
Only they shone with beauty, for they were like themselves.
They appeared to me a long, long time, and happily.

I woke up. I opened my eyes.
I touched the world as if it were a carved frame.

MARINA TSVETAYEVA

from The Bus

Translated by Elaine Feinstein

The bus jumped, like a brazen
evil spirit,   a demon
cutting across the traffic
in streets as cramped as footnotes,
it rushed on its way   shaking
like a concert-hall vibrating
with applause.   And we shook in it!
Demons too.   Have you seen
seeds under a tap? We were
like peas in boiling soup,
or Easter toys dancing in
alcohol.   Mortared grain!
Teeth in a chilled mouth.

What   has been shaken out   someone
could use for a chandelier:
all the beads   and the bones
of an old woman. A necklace
on that girl's breast. Bouncing.
The child at his mother's nipple.
Shaken without reference.
Like pears   all of us   shaken
in *vibrato*, like violins.
The violence shook our souls
into laughter, and back into childhood.

A Memory

This is just the weather, a wet May and blowing,
   All the shining, shimmering leaves tossing low and high,
When my father used to say: ''Twill be the great mowing!
   God's weather's a good weather, be it wet or dry.'

Blue were his eyes and his cheeks were so ruddy,
   He was out in all weathers, up and down the farm;
With the pleasant smile and the word for a wet body;
   'Sure, the weather's God's weather. Who can take the harm?'

With a happy word he'd silence all repining
   While the hay lay wet in field and the cattle died,
When the rain rained every day and no sun was shining,
   'Ah, well, God is good,' he'd say, even while he sighed.

In the parched summer with the corn not worth saving,
   Every field bare as your hand and the beasts to feed,
Still he kept his heart up, while other folk were raving:
   'God will send the fodder: 'tis He that knows the need.'

A wet May, a wild May; he used to rise up cheery
   In the grey of the morning for market and for fair.
Now he sleeps the whole year long, though days be bright, be dreary,
   In God's weather that's good weather he sleeps without a care.

Now, 'tis just the weather, a wild May and weeping,
   How the blackbird sang and sang 'mid the tossing leaves!
When my father used to say: ''Twill be the great reaping:
   God send fine weather to carry home the sheaves!'

JEAN VALENTINE

Alone, Alive

Alone, alive
with you
more alone
more alive
open open
to and from
the bloodwarm breast
the nest you were born to
the eye the hair
the window the light. Light
the astronauts saw
and grew full of trepidation,
softer,
and more full of life.

My window
my cove
my trout
my flood
my green trepidation
my mushroom
my tongue
my salt my moon
my moon my sun
I lay down my
spear
before your light
your eye
your hair.

To A Stranger

Passing stranger! you do not know how longingly I look upon you,
You must be he I was seeking, or she I was seeking, (it comes to me
  as of a dream),
I have somewhere surely lived a life of joy with you,
All is recall'd as we flit by each other, fluid, affectionate, chaste,
  matured,
You grew up with me, were a boy with me or a girl with me,
I ate with you and slept with you, your body has become not yours
  only nor left my body mine only,
You give me the pleasure of your eyes, face, flesh, as we pass, you
  take of my beard, breast, hands, in return,
I am not to speak to you, I am to think of you when I sit alone or
  wake at night alone,
I am to wait, I do not doubt I am to meet you again,
I am to see to it that I do not lose you.

OSCAR WILDE

Requiescat

Tread lightly, she is near
    Under the snow,
Speak gently, she can hear
    The daisies grow.

All her bright golden hair
    Tarnished with rust,
She that was young and fair
    Fallen to dust.

Lily-like, white as snow,
    She hardly knew
She was a woman, so
    Sweetly she grew.

Coffin-board, heavy stone
    Lie on her breast,
I vex my heart alone,
    She is at rest.

Peace, Peace, she cannot hear
    Lyre or sonnet,
All my life's buried here,
    Heap earth upon it.

WILLIAM CARLOS WILLIAMS

The Sun

lifts heavily
and cloud and sea
weigh upon the
unwaiting air—

Hasteless
the silence is
divided
by small waves

that wash away
night whose wave
is without
sound and gone—

Old categories
slacken
memoryless—
weed and shells where

in the night
a high tide left
its mark
and block of half

burned wood washed
clean—
The slovenly bearded
rocks hiss—

Obscene refuse
charms
this modern shore—
Listen!

it is a sea-snail
singing—
Relax, relent—
the sun has climbed

the sand is
drying—Lie
by the broken boat—
the eel-grass

bends
and is released
again—Go down, go
down past knowledge

shelly lace—
among the rot
of children
screaming

their delight—
logged
in the penetrable
nothingness

whose heavy body
opens
to their leaps
without a wound—

November

November
and the tail-end of a hurricane
it seems strange

at the end of it all

at the last home
I wait here to welcome you

grey day
at the unexplored end
of Ranelagh—

down by the brimming river
I heard . . .
there is a tree
that grows aslant a brook

where murderers
lure children
disused railway tracks
back lanes
and river paths

we drown
and all our stories
wash
down-river to the sea

I must
take up the story once again

In nineteen forty-six
or seven
in Pembroke Street
you said
you would humiliate me
for taking

a couple of walnuts
from a shop display

and many a time you did

one way and another
of all mothers
one's own is the maddest

Will you
embarrass me today—

what can I say
for you
long since
gone into
a country of the mind
where I can't speak
protect you
or protect myself

MÁIRÍDE WOODS

Sunday Outing

Once in the car I wish we were going
Anywhere but here. From the empty backseat
Drift all the sunlit, squabbling, half-squashed
Hours we spent
En route to family life.

The uphill struggle with your chair
Across rough fields to off-key summer fêtes;
That freezing circus with the ghastly clowns;
If I could put a sticky finger
On any one of them. . . .

Past the iron gates, our new world
Is all happy families. Beloved mothers,
Peerless dads lie tucked in stone rectangles. Our plot
Is still unfenced and waterlogged,
Raw to the sky.

We carry rosemary and mint
A comfort scent-blanket from home
For the other world. I try my trowel
On clay and stone, knowing not even mother-love
Can bring you back.

But dereliction isn't possible. We toss old wreaths
Into the yellow skip. Greying roses, chrysanths,
—At least they self-destruct
Unlike your clothes and all your deadlines
Still sounding in my mind.

The best-kept graves, I see
Belong to little children. Silly windmills
Fidget through picket fences; and parents
Like great bedraggled birds
Pecking at dust.

VINCENT WOODS

After The American Wake

It is 1904 or 1905—we don't know the time of year
        but it's likely summer.
Two men say goodbye forever at a green gate
        over a stream.
They are both called Myles, both are tall and thin.
        One is going to America
                and will never return
        One is staying here
                and will never leave.

They have watched the dawn rise over the lough,
        seen the last of the stragglers home.
They hear the jingle of the horse's harness, linger,
        Clasp hands, hear the driver shout.
Remember, said the one leaving, Remember tonight.

William Wordsworth

Surprised by joy—impatient as the Wind

Surprised by joy—impatient as the Wind
I turned to share the transport—Oh! with whom
But Thee, deep buried in the silent tomb,
That spot which no vicissitude can find?
Love, faithful love, recalled thee to my mind—
But how could I forget thee? Through what power,
Even for the least division of an hour,
Have I been so beguiled as to be blind
To my most grievous loss!—That thought's return
Was the worst pang that sorrow ever bore,
Save one, one only, when I stood forlorn,
Knowing my heart's best treasure was no more;
That neither present time, nor years unborn
Could to my sight that heavenly face restore.

They fle from me that sometyme did me seke

They fle from me that sometyme did me seke
  With naked fote stalking in my chambre.
I have sene theim gentill tame and meke
  That nowe are wyld and do not remembre
  That sometyme they put theimself in daunger
To take bred at my hand; and nowe they raunge
Besely seking with a continuell chaunge.

Thancked be fortune, it hath ben othrewise
  Twenty tymes better; but ons in speciall,
In thyn arraye after a pleasaunt gyse,
  When her lose gowne from her shoulders did fall,
  And she me caught in her armes long and small;
Therewithall swetely did me kysse,
And softely saide, *dere hert, howe like you this?*

It was no dreme: I lay brode waking.
  But all is torned thorough my gentilnes
Into a straunge fasshion of forsaking;
  And I have leve to goo of her goodenes,
  And she also to vse new fangilnes.
But syns that I so kyndely ame serued,
I would fain knowe what she hath deserued.

ENDA WYLEY

Dish of a Moon

For Martin Drury

'But then it's the light
that makes you remember.'

Yehuda Amichai, *Forgetting Someone*

I get up to pace the house late at night—
am an anxious adult shutting the doors, winding the clock,
pulling out plugs, making the dripping tap stop;
but on the landing, I look out to check the light,

neighbours' roof-tops, my trees, the weather.
Wind tugs at the moon that is a memory
wide and yellow and I am a tide of worry
dragged back again to what I will never forget—my mother

kneeling beside me, her six year old child, mopping
my night-time sweats away with her sweet made-up tune.
Lady Moon, Lady Moon, she sings to the high dish of a moon—
nearly forty years on, I swear I can still hear her singing

and feel her arm tight around me, her finger
pointing down below to two foxes who have found their way
into our garden through the wood of time. Their eyes looking up, say
the moon is a light left on—its light there to make you remember.

W. B. Yeats

Adam's Curse

We sat together at one summer's end,
That beautiful mild woman, your close friend,
And you and I, and talked of poetry.
I said, 'A line will take us hours maybe;
Yet if it does not seem a moment's thought,
Our stitching and unstitching has been naught.
Better go down upon your marrow-bones
And scrub a kitchen pavement, or break stones
Like an old pauper, in all kinds of weather;
For to articulate sweet sounds together
Is to work harder than all these, and yet
Be thought an idler by the noisy set
Of bankers, schoolmasters and clergymen
The martyrs call the world.'

                And thereupon
That beautiful mild woman for whose sake
There's many a one shall find out all heartache
On finding that her voice is sweet and low
Replied, 'To be born woman is to know—
Although they do not talk of it at school—
That we must labour to be beautiful.'

I said, 'It's certain there is no fine thing
Since Adam's fall but needs much labouring.
There have been lovers who thought love should be
So much compounded of high courtesy
That they would sigh and quote with learned looks
Precedents out of beautiful old books;
Yet now it seems an idle trade enough.'

We sat grown quiet at the name of love;
We saw the last embers of daylight die,
And in the trembling blue-green of the sky
A moon, worn as if it had been a shell
Washed by time's waters as they rose and fell
About the stars and broke in days and years.
I had a thought for no one's but your ears:
That you were beautiful, and that I strove
To love you in the old high way of love;
That it had all seemed happy, and yet we'd grown
As weary-hearted as that hollow moon.

The poets

Fleur Adcock was born in New Zealand but has lived in England since 1963. Her collected poems, now out of print, have been replaced by *Poems 1960–2000*.

Sherman Alexie is a Spokane/Coeur d'Alene Indian. His most recent book of poems is *One Stick Song*.

Nuala Archer was born of Irish parents in New York in 1955. Her poetry collections are *Whale on the Line* (1981) and *From a Mobile Home*, both published by Salmon.

Ingeborg Bachmann (1926–1973) grew up in Klagenfort, a small Austrian city near the Yugoslavian and Italian borders. 'A Kind of Loss' is taken from *In the Storm of Roses*, a bilingual edition of her work.

Ivy Bannister is the author of *Magician*, a collection of short stories. She lives in Dublin.

Leland Bardwell is the author of four collections of poetry. Her most recent one is *The White Beach* (1998). Her latest novel is *Mother to a Stranger* (2002). She is a member of Aosdána.

Sara Berkeley was born in Dublin in 1967. She is the author of three collections of poetry, a collection of short stories, and a novel, *Shadowing Hannah* (1999). She now lives in Northern California.

Eavan Boland was born in Dublin in 1944. Her *Collected Poems* appeared in 1995. Her most recent books are *Code* and *The Making of a Poem: The Norton Anthology of Poetic Forms,* which she co-edited with Mark Strand.

Lucy Brennan was born in Dublin in 1931 and emigrated to Canada in 1957. Her first collection, *Migrants All*, was published in Toronto in 1999.

Catherine Byron grew up in Belfast, farmed in Scotland, and now lives in the English Midlands. Her sixth poetry collection is *The Getting of Vellum* (2000).

Louise C. Callaghan was born in 1948 in Shankill, Co. Dublin. Her poetry collection *The Puzzle-Heart* was published in 1999.

Mary Rose Callan was born in Sligo and now lives in Dublin. Her collection is *The Mermaid's Head* (2001).

Siobhán Campbell has published two collections of poetry: *The

Permanent Wave (1996) and most recently, *the cold that burns* (2000). She lives in Dublin with her family.

Moya Cannon was born in Dunfanaghy, Co. Donegal and lives in Galway. Her most recent collections are *Oar* (1990) and *The Parchment Boat* (1997).

Philip Casey has published three collections, including *The Year of the Knife* (1990), and three novels, including *The Fisher Child* (2001). He is a member of Aosdána, and lives in Dublin.

Paul Celan was born in 1920 in Czernowitz, which is now in Romania. His parents, German-speaking Jews, died in Nazi labour camps. He lived most of his adult life in Paris. He committed suicide by drowning in 1970.

John Clare (1793–1864) was born and raised in rural Northamptonshire. His first collection, *Poems Descriptive of Rural Life and Scenery*, was highly acclaimed. He died in poverty in Northampton General Lunatic Asylum.

Austin Clarke (1896–1974) was born in Dublin. He published more than 30 works of poetry, drama and criticism. He was awarded a D. Litt. from Trinity College Dublin as 'the outstanding literary figure in modern Ireland'.

Susan Connolly lives in Drogheda, Co. Louth. Her collection *For the Stranger* was published in 1993. In 2001 she won the Patrick and Katherine Kavanagh Fellowship in Poetry. Her second collection, *A Salmon in the Pool,* awaits publication.

Colette Connor was born and currently lives in Dublin. Her work has appeared in *Poetry Ireland Review*.

Roz Cowman lives and works in Cork. She received the Patrick Kavanagh Award in 1985.

E.E. Cummings (1894–1962) was born in Cambridge, Massachussetts and educated at Harvard University. His *Complete Poems 1923–1954* came out in 1975.

Seamus Deane's most recent publications are the Booker-shortlisted novel *Reading in the Dark* (1996) and *Future Crossings* (2000) which he co-edited with K. Ziarek.

Celia de Fréine, playwright and poet, lives in Dublin. A first collection, *Faoi Chabáistí is Ríonacha* was published by Cló Iar-Chonnachta in 2001.

Greg Delanty was born in Cork in 1958 and now lives in Vermont. His latest volumes of poetry are *The Hellbox* (1998), *The Blind Stitch* (2001), and *The Ship of Birth* (2003).

Emily Dickinson (1830–1866) lived and died in her father's house in Amherst, Massachussets. A recluse for most of her life, she wrote over 1,700 poems. A complete edition was published in 1956.

Mary Dorcey was born in 1950 and grew up in Dalkey, Co. Dublin. She has published four collections of poetry. The latest is *Like Joy in Season, Like Sorrow* (1998).

Carol Ann Duffy was born in Glasgow in 1955. Recent collections include *The World's Wife* (1999) and *Feminine Gospels* (2002).

Paul Durcan was born in Dublin in 1944. His most recent book of poems is *Cries of an Irish Caveman* (2001). He has published over fifteen books of poetry, among them *Greetings to Our Friends in Brazil* (1999).

Peter Fallon was born in Germany in 1951. Founder of The Gallery Press, he lives in Co. Meath. He published *News of the World: Selected and New Poems* in 1993.

Lawrence Ferlinghetti is the first Poet Laureate of San Francisco. He has published books through his company, City Lights Books, for over forty years.

Tess Gallagher is a poet, short story writer, and essayist. *My Black Horse: New & Selected Poems* was published in 1995.

Elizabeth Grainger lives in New York City. Her work has appeared in journals including *The Paris Review* and *Poetry*.

Robert Greacen, a member of Aosdána, has published many books of both prose and poetry. His *Collected Poems* won the Irish Times Poetry Prize in 1995.

Angela Greene (1936–1997) was born in England but grew up in Dublin. She lived and died in Drogheda. Her only collection is *Silence and the Blue Night*.

Thom Gunn was born in England in 1929. He moved to the USA in 1954 and has spent most of his writing life in Northern California. His recent books include *The Man With Night Sweats*, *Collectd Poems* and *Boss Cupid*.

Kerry Hardie was born in 1951. Her works include *A Furious Place* (1996), *Cry for the Hot Belly* (2000), *The Sky Didn't Fall* (2003), and two novels.

Anne Le Marquand Hartigan is a poet, playwright and painter. She has published four collections of poetry as well as a prose meditation on creativity, *Clearing the Space* (1996).

Michael Hartnett was born in Newcastle West, Co. Limerick in 1941. In 1975 he published *A Farewell to English*. His *Collected Poems* came out in 2001 after his death.

Anne Haverty's *The Beauty of the Moon* was published in 1999. Other publications include the novels *One Day as a Tiger* and *The Far Side of a Kiss*. She was born in Holycross, Co. Tipperary in 1959 and now lives in Dublin.

H. D. (1886–1961) was born Hilda Doolittle in Bethlehem, Pennsylvania. In 1911 she went to England and never returned to America. Her volumes of poetry include *Sea Garden* and *Helen in Egypt*.

Seamus Heaney was born in Co. Derry in 1939. He has published poetry, criticism and translations which were saluted by the award of the Nobel Prize for Literature in 1995. His most recent book of poems is *Electric Light* (2001).

Rita Ann Higgins was born in 1955 in Galway. Author of seven collections of poetry, her most recent publications include *Sunny Side Plucked—New and Selected Poems* (1996), and *An Awful Racket* (2001).

Ellen Hinsey is the author of *Cities of Memory* (1996), which was awarded the Yale Series of Younger Poets Prize in 1996, and *The White Fire of Time* (2002).

Pearse Hutchinson, poet and translator, was born in Glasgow in 1927. He is co-editor of *Cyphers* and a member of Aosdána. He published his *Collected Poems* in 2002.

Biddy Jenkinson's most recent book of poetry is *Mis*, published by Coiscéim in 2001. She likes to write plays and stories when she can't write poems.

Patrick Kavanagh (1904–1967) was born in Co. Monaghan, son of a small farmer. He eventually settled in Dublin. His long poem *The Great Hunger* (1942) is considered his finest work. A *Selected Poems* was published in 1996.

Jackie Kay was born in Scotland in 1961. Her first collection is *The Adoption Papers* (1991). She is also author of two novels, *Trumpet* (1999) and *The Straw Girl* (2002).

John Keats (1795–1820) entered Guy's Hospital as a medical student, though he never completed his studies. He died in Italy of tuberculosis at the early age of twenty-five.

D. H. Lawrence (1885–1930) was born in Nottinghamshire, the fourth son of a coalminer. He is mainly renowned for his novels.

Michael Longley was born in Belfast in 1939. His collection *The Weather in Japan* won both the Hawthornden Prize and the T. S. Eliot prize for 2000.

James J. McAuley was born in Dublin in 1936. His ninth collection of poems, *Meditations, With Distractions,* was published in 2001. He now lives in West Wicklow.

Joan McBreen edited *The White Page/An Bhileog Bán, Irish Women Poets* (1999). Her collections include *The Wind Beyond the Wall* (1990) and *New & Selected Poems* (2003).

Catherine Phil MacCarthy has published two collections of poetry, *This Hour of the Tide* (1994) and *The Blue Globe* (1998). She has recently completed her first novel, *One Room an Everywhere* (2003).

Medbh McGuckian was born and lives in Belfast. Her latest collections are *Drawing Ballerinas* (2001) and *Had I a Thousand Lives* (2003).

Frank McGuinness grew up in Buncrana, Co. Donegal. He has published three collections of poetry: *Booterstown* (1994), *The Sea with no Ships* (1999) and *The Stone Jug* (2003) and many plays.

Derek Mahon was born in Belfast in 1941 and grew up there. As critic Edna Longley remarked 'Belfast and the Antrim coast shaped his imaginative spirit'. His *Collected Poems* was published in 1999.

José Martí (1853–1895) was born in Cuba, of Spanish parents. He became involved in the struggle for Cuban liberation, which led to his eventual deportation to Madrid. *Ismaelillo*, his first poetry collection, was published in 1882.

Aidan Mathews grew up in Dublin where he now livews with his family. Besides writing for the theatre he has published short stories and three collections of poetry.

Caitlín Maude (1941–1982) was born in Rosmuc in the Conamara Gaeltacht. Her poems are gathered in one volume, *Caitlín Maude, Dánta* (1984).

Máighréad Medbh was born in Limerick in 1959. Much of her work is performance poetry. Her latest collection is called *Tenant* (1999).

Paula Meehan was born in 1955 and grew up in Dublin's inner city. *Dharmakaya* (2000) is the latest of her seven books of poetry. She is among the trio represented in *Three Irish Poets: An Anthology* (Carcanet: 2003).

Áine Miller was born in Cork. Her first collection is *Goldfish in a Baby Bath* (1994).

Noel Monahan has published three collections of poetry: *Opposite Walls* (1991), *Snowfire* (1995), and *Curse of the Birds* (2000), all published by Salmon Publishing.

John Montague, was born in 1929 in Brooklyn of Ulster parents. His *Collected Poems* (1995) were followed by *Smashing the Piano* (1999) and *Selected Poems* (2001).

Ágnes Nemes Nagy was born in Budapest in 1922. His principal collections are *Dry Lightening* (1957), *Solstice* (1967) and *Transformation of a Railway Station* (1980).

Pablo Neruda (1904–1973), a Nobel Laureate, was born in Parral, Chile. His most famous poem is the epic 'Canto General'. He served briefly under President Allende as Chilean Ambassador to Paris.

Eiléan Ní Chuilleanáin was born in Cork in 1942. Her most recent collection is *The Girl who Married the Reindeer* (2001). She is married to poet Macdara Woods and lives in Dublin.

Nuala Ní Dhomhnaill was born in England in 1952 and raised in the Gaeltacht of Co. Kerry. *The Water Horse* is her most recent collection. It has bilingual translations by Medbh McGuckian and Eiléan Ní Chuilleanáin.

Julie O'Callaghan was born in Chicago and writes poetry for children and adults. Her most recent collection, *No Can Do* (2000), won the Michael Hartnett Poetry Award for 2001.

John O'Donnell was born in Dublin in 1956. His first collection is *Some Other Country* (2002).

Dennis O'Driscoll, born in Thurles in 1954, has published five collections of poetry, including *Weather Permitting* (1999) and *Exemplary Damages* (2002). A selection of his prose writings, *Troubled Thoughts, Majestic Dreams* was published in 2001.

Sheila O'Hagan was born in 1933 and raised in Dublin. Her collections include *The Peacock's Eye* (1992) and *The Troubled House* (1995).

Caitríona O'Reilly was born in Dublin in 1973. Her debut collection of poetry, *The Nowhere Birds,* was published in 2001.

Cathal Ó Searcaigh was born in Co. Donegal in 1956. His Irish language poetry is widely translated. He is the author of ten collections of poems. He is a member of Aosdána. His latest collection is *Ag tnúth leis an tSolas* (2000).

Antonia Pozzi (1902–1928) was born in Milan but spent much of her childhood in the countryside of Pasturo in east Lombardy. She committed suicide at the age of twenty six.

Minnie Bruce Pratt's books include *Crime Against Nature* (1989), *We Say We Love Each Other* (1992) and *Walking Back Up Depot Street* (1999).

Adrienne Rich is one of North America's foremost poets. Her most recent books are *Arts of the Possible: Essays and Conversations* (2001) and *Fox: Poems 1998–2001* (2001).

Rainer Maria Rilke (1875–1926) was born in Prague. His first book of poetry, *Leben und Lieder,* was published when he was just 19 years old. He was briefly married to the sculptor Klara Westhoff.

Christina Rossetti (1830–1894) was born in London, the younger sister of the painter and poet Dante Gabriel Rossetti.

Nelly Sachs (1891–1970) was born in Berlin, but in 1940 escaped with other Jews to Stockholm, where she lived for the rest of her life. In 1966 she was awarded the Nobel Prize for Literature. *O, the Chimneys* (1967) and *The Seeker and Other Poems* (1970) are available in English translation.

William Shakespeare (1564–1616) is widely regarded as the greatest poet in the English language. As well as over thirty plays, he wrote two long poems and a sequence of 150 sonnets.

Charles Simic was born in Yugoslavia in 1938 and emigrated with his family to the USA when he was eleven years old. His first book was *Dismantling the Silence* (1971).

Jo Slade was born in England in 1952 and educated in Limerick. Her collections include *In Fields I Hear Them Sing* (1989) and *Certain Octobers—Parfois en Octobre* (1997).

Gary Snyder is the author of seventeen books of poetry, including *No Nature* and recently *High Sierra*. He lives in the northern Sierra of California.

Edith Södergran (1892–1923) grew up in Ravola, a village on the Fino-Russian border. She was Finnish but wrote her intensely visionary poems, in Swedish. Her *Complete Poems* are translated by David McDuff (1984).

Anne Stevenson, born in 1933 of American parents was brought up in the USA but has lived for most of her life in England, Scotland and Wales. Her eight collections include *The Collected Poems, 1955–1995*.

Eithne Strong (1923–1999) was born in west Co. Leitrim. She received her education in the Gaeltacht. She continued to publish poetry in English and Irish into her eighth decade.

Wislawa Szymborska was born in 1928 in Poland in the Poznan region. She won the Nobel Prize for Literature in 1996. Her most recent book is *View with a Grain of Sand: Selected Poems* (1995). She lives in Cracow.

Marina Tsvetayeva (1892–1941) was born in Moscow. She published her first volume of poetry before she was twenty. She lived mostly in exile after the Russian Revolution. In the Soviet Union in 1941, she took her own life.

Katherine Tynan (1861–1931) was born in Dublin and grew up in Clondalkin. Widowed in 1919, she made her living by writing. She was a prominent member of the Irish Literary Revival.

Jean Valentine was born in Chicago in 1934. Her most recent book is *The Cradle of Real Life* (2000). She lives in New York City.

Walt Whitman (1819–1892) grew up in the state of New York. *Leaves of Grass*, his best known book, celebrates democracy, comradeship and American life.

Oscar Wilde (1854–1900) was born in Dublin. He studied classics and won a scholarship to Oxford University. His poetry (which includes *The Ballad of Reading Gaol*) is eclipsed by his more famous work as a playwright.

William Carlos Williams (1883–1963) was a medical doctor as well as a poet. His career in both medicine and poetry spanned six decades.

Macdara Woods was born in Dublin. He has published thirteen books, mostly poetry, as well as musical collaborations. His two most recent collections are *Knowledge in the Blood* (2000), and *The Nightingale Water* (2001). He is married to Eiléan Ní Chuileanáin and is a member of Aosdána.

Máiríde Woods is a long struggling writer of poetry and short stories many of which have been broadcast on radio. She lives in North Dublin with her family.

Vincent Woods was born in Co. Leitrim in 1960. His plays include *At the Black Pig's Dyke* and his poetry *The Colour of Language*. He has co-edited *The Turning Wake: Poems and Songs of Irish Australia* (2001).

William Wordsworth (1770–1850) was born in England. Along with S. T. Coleridge, he spearheaded the Romantic movement in English poetry with the collection *Lyrical Ballads*. He was made Poet Laureate in 1843.

Sir Thomas Wyatt (1503–1542) was surpassed as a love poet only by Spenser and Shakespeare.

Enda Wyley was born in Dublin in 1966. She has published two collections of poetry, *Eating Baby Jesus* (1994) and *Socrates in the Garden* (1998).

W. B. Yeats (1865–1939) grew up in Dublin, Sligo and London. He led the Irish Literary Revival of the late nineteenth and early twentieth centuries and supported the movement for Irish independence. He won the Nobel Prize for Literature in 1923.

A. & A. Farmar would like to thank all the authors (or their estates), translators, agents and publishers for their assistance in publishing this anthology and particularly for their generosity in waiving their usual fees in favour of the Alzheimer Society of Ireland. Thanks are due, too, to Eithne Jordan for allowing us to reproduce her painting 'Beachscape at Noon' on the cover. Every effort has been made to trace copyright-holders. If any have been overlooked the publishers would be grateful to be contacted. Permission to use copyright material is gratefully acknowledged as follows.

'Indian Boy Love Songs' is reprinted from *The Business of Fancydancing* © 1992 by Sherman Alexie, by permission of Hanging Loose Press.

Ingeborg Bachmann 'A Kind of Loss', translated by Mark Anderson, is from *In the Storm of Roses: Selected Poems* (1986), with kind permission of Piper Verlag.

'Recall' is reprinted from *the cold that burns* © 2000 by Siobhán Campbell by kind permission of the Blackstaff Press.

Paul Celan 'Corona' is taken from *Poems of Paul Celan* translated by Michael Hamburger. Published by Anvil Press Poetry in 1988. © Suhrkamp Verlag, Frankfurt am Main, 1967, 1968, 1970, 1971, 1976.

Extract from 'Mnemosyne Lay in Dust' by Austin Clarke from *Collected Poems* (1974) is reprinted by kind permission of R. Dardis Clarke, 21 Pleasants Street, Dublin 8.

'in time of daffodils(who know' is reprinted from *Complete Poems 1904–1962* by E.E. Cummings, edited by George J. Firmage, by permission of W. W. Norton & Company. Copyright © 1991 by the Trustees for the E.E. Cummings Trust and George James Firmage.

'Stafford Afternoons' is taken from *Mean Time* by Carol Ann Duffy published by Anvil Press Poetry in 1993.

'Pictures of the Gone World' is reprinted from *City Lights Pocket Poets Anthology* (1994) by kind permission of Lawrence Ferlinghetti.

'Memory Unsettled' from *The Man With Night Sweats* (1992) by Thom Gunn is reprinted by kind permission of Faber & Faber.

'The Ash Plant' from *Seeing Things* (1991) by Seamus Heaney is reprinted by kind permission of Faber & Faber.

'On a Visit to Budapest' from *Cities of Memory* (1996) by Ellen Hinsey is reproduced by kind permission of Yale University Press.

'15 Eanáir 1991' from *Rogha Dánta* (2000) © Biddy Jenkinson. Reproduced by permission of Cork University Press, Crawford Business Park, Crosses Green, Cork, Ireland.

'October' by Patrick Kavanagh is reprinted from *Selected Poems*, edited by Antoinette Quinn (Penguin Books, 1996), with the permission of the Trustees of the Estate of the late Katherine B. Kavanagh, through the Jonathan Williams Literary Agency.

'Piano' from *The Complete Poems of D. H. Lawrence* (1977) is reprinted by kind permission of Laurence Pollinger Limited and the Estate of Frieda Lawrence Ravagli.

'Memory' is reprinted from *Selected Poems by Pablo Neruda* (1975), translated by Alastair Reid, edited by Nathaniel Tarn and published by Jonathan Cape. Used by permission of The Random House Group Limited.

'Scéala/Annunciations' from *Selected Poems* (2000) by Nuala Ní Dhomhnaill is reprinted by kind permission of New Island Books.

'Deadlines' is taken from *Weather Permitting* by Dennis O'Driscoll published by Anvil Press Poetry in 1999.

'For Memory' is reprinted from *A Wild Patience Has Taken Me This Far: Poems 1978–1981* (1981) by Adrienne Rich. Copyright © by Adrienne Rich. Used by permission of the

dom House Group Ltd. 'The Branch' from *The Weather in Japan* (2000) by Michael Longley published by Jonathan Cape. Used by permission of The Random House Group Ltd. Gary Snyder 'Ripples on the Surface' from *No Nature* (1992).

The following poems are reprinted by kind permission of Salmon Publishing: 'No Return' from *The White Beach* (1998) by Leland Bardwell; 'The Blue Darkness' from *The Getting of Vellum* (2000) by Catherine Byron; 'Dream of the Red Chamber' from *The Goose Herd* (1989) by Roz Cowman; 'Elegy' from *Silence and the Blue Night* (1993) by Angela Greene; 'Leaving' from *Now is a Moveable Feast* (1991) by Anne Le Marquand Hartigan; 'Birth Mother' from *This Hour of the Tide* (1994) by Catherine Phil MacCarthy; 'In the garden at Barna' from *Goldfish in a Baby Bath* (1994) by Áine Miller; 'In School' from *Curse of the Birds* (2000) by Noel Monahan; 'Welcome' from *Let Live* (1990) by Eithne Strong; 'The Wood Pigeon' from *The Troubled House* (1995) by Sheila O'Hagan; 'Girl' from *A Walled Garden in Moylough* (1995) by Joan McBreen; 'Expulsion: A Foetal Hymn' from *The Vigilant One* (1994) by Jo Slade; 'At Every Window a Different Season' from *The River That Carries Me* (1995) by Mary Dorcey .

'Adam's Curse' is reprinted from *The Collected Poems of W. B. Yeats*, (Macmillan & Co., 1958) by kind permission of Dr Michael Yeats. 'After The American Wake' by Vincent Woods and 'Benediction' by Pearse Hutchinson are reprinted from *Cyphers 49–50*. 'Aimhréidhe' by Caitlín Maude is reprinted from *Caitlín Maude, Dánta* (Coiscéim, 1984) by kind permission of Cathal Ó Luain. 'Alone, Alive' by Jean Valentine is reprinted from *The river at wolf* (Alice James Books, 1992). 'At Brendan Behan's Desk' by Robert Greacen is reprinted from *Fortnight Magazine* (344, November 1995). 'Return' by Seamus Deane is reprinted from *Gradual Wars* (Irish Academic Press, 1972). 'Death of a Season' by Antonia Pozzi is reprinted from *Italian Poets of the Twentieth Century* (Irish Academic Press, 1996). 'Done' by Minnie Bruce Pratt is reprinted from *We Say We Love Each Other* (Firebrand Books, 1992). 'Hermetic Definitions' by H. D. (Hilda Doolittle) is reprinted from *Collected Poems 1912–1944* (New Directions, 1983). 'I Am' by John Clare is reprinted from *The Penguin Book of English Verse* (Penguin, 1956). 'Landscapes with Interior' by James J. McAuley is reprinted from *Meditations, with Distractions* (University of Arkanas Press, 2001). 'Little Horseman' is a translation by Louise C. Callaghan of 'Mi Caballero' by José Martí from *Ismaelillo* (Mondadori, 1999). 'Mullaghbawn 1950' by Lucy Brennan is reprinted from *Migrants All* (WatershedBooks, 1999). 'Poor Lily' by Colette Connor is reprinted from *Chapman* (Irish issue 92, 1999). 'Surprised by joy—impatient as the Wind' by William Wordsworth is reprinted from *The Essential Wordsworth*. 'They fle from me that sometyme did me seke' by Sir Thomas Wyatt is reprinted from *Collected Poems of Sir Thomas Wyatt*. ' To a Stranger' by Walt Whitman is reprinted from *Leaves of Grass*. 'You cannot make Remembrance grow' by Emily Dickinson is reprinted from *Emily Dickinson: The Complete Poems*. 'The Good X' by Elizabeth Grainger is from an unpublished collection 'Women and Animals'. 'In drear-nighted December' by John Keats is reprinted from *Selected Poems and Letters of John Keats* (Heinemann, 1976).

Index of titles